CONCILIUM

Religion in the Eighties

CONCILIUM

Editorial Directors

Concilium 175 (5/1984): Sacred Scripture

CONCILIUM

CONCILIUM

List of Members

Advisory Committee: Dogma

CONCILIUM

List of Members

Advisory Committee: Ecumenism

Directors:

Hans Küng	Tübingen	West Germany
Jürgen Moltmann	Tübingen	West Germany

Members:

Arthur Allchin	Canterbury	Great Britain
René Beaupère OP	Lyons	France
Robert Clément SJ	Beirut	Lebanon
Avery Dulles SJ	Washington, DC	USA
André Dumas	Paris	France
Herman Fiolet	Bilthoven	The Netherlands
Alexandre Ganoczy	Würzburg	West Germany
Manuel Gesteira Garza	Madrid	Spain
Hermann Häring	Bedbürg-Hau	West Germany
Michael Hurley SJ	Dublin	Ireland
Walter Kasper	Tübingen	West Germany
Bernard Lambert OP	Courville	Canada
Emmanuel Lanne OSB	Chevetogne	Belgium
Hervé Legrand OP	Paris	France
Peter Lengsfeld	Münster-Hiltrup	West Germany
Joseph Lescrauwaet MSC	Louvain	Belgium
George Lindbeck	New Haven, Conn.	USA
Hendrik van der Linde	Berg en Dal	The Netherlands
Jan Milic Lochman	Basel	Switzerland
Antonio Matabosch	Barcelona	Spain
Harry McSorley	Toronto, Ont.	Canada
John Meyendorff	Tuckahoe, NY	USA
José Miguez Bonino	Buenos Aires	Argentine
Ronald Modras	St Louis, Mo.	USA
Nikos Nissiotis	Ilissia-Athens	Greece
John Oesterreicher	South Orange, NJ	USA
Daniel O'Hanlon SJ	Berkeley, Cal.	USA
Wolfhart Pannenberg	Gräfelfing	West Germany
Otto Pesch	Hamburg	West Germany
Alfonso Skowronek	Warsaw	Poland
Heinrich Stirnimann	Fribourg	Switzerland
Gustave Thils	Louvain	Belgium
Lukas Vischer	Berne	Switzerland
Willem de Vries SJ	Rome	Italy
Jan Witte SJ	Rome	Italy

THE
HOLOCAUST
AS
INTERRUPTION

Edited by
Elisabeth Schüssler Fiorenza
and
David Tracy

English Language Editor ·
Marcus Lefébure

T. & T. CLARK LTD
Edinburgh

October 1984
T. & T. Clark Ltd, 36 George Street, Edinburgh EH2 2LQ
ISBN: 0 567 30055 2

ISSN: 0010-5236

Typeset by C. R. Barber & Partners (Highlands) Ltd, Fort William
Printed in Scotland by Blackwood, Pillans & Wilson Ltd, Edinburgh

Concilium: Published February, April, June, August, October, December.
Subscriptions 1984: USA: US$40.00 (including air mail postage and packing); Canada:
Canadian$50.00 (including air mail postage and packing); UK and rest of the world:
£19.00 (including postage and packing).

CONTENTS

Part IV
Inter-disciplinary Reflections

Part V
Editorial Reflections

Editorial

AS CHRISTIAN theology moves past a concern for historical consciousness alone or even historicity alone into concrete history, it finds itself facing the frightening interruption of the Holocaust.

'History' can no longer be understood as linearity nor continuity, much less evolutionary optimism. Theologically construed, history is concrete: here the concrete suffering of peoples trapped in the horror of the Holocaust. When facing *that* event, history theologically becomes interruption.

Theologians come to the issue of the Holocaust not to 'explain' it but to face it—and to face it theologically. The present issue is one attempt to have different theologians and other thinkers address this issue and be addressed by it.

In the first section we turn first, as we Christian theologians should, to our Jewish colleagues: here two Jewish thinkers, Susan Shapiro and Arthur Cohen. Susan Shapiro provides important hermeneutical reflections on the testimonies to the event while Arthur Cohen develops his well-known theological reflections on the *tremendum* for this issue.

In the second section we turn to Christian theological reflections on the event of the Holocaust. Each of our theologians provides a new focus for the kind of Christian theological reflections that are now needed by the whole Christian community.

The third section allows for further analyses of this event of interruption in biblical studies. Luise Schottroff demonstrates the concrete exegetical issues at stake in New Testament research and shows, through a case study of German Christian exegesis during the horrors of the Nazi period the frightening reality of anti-Judaism that can prevail in official Christian exegesis and theology.

In a fourth section, we turn to the consequences of this event of interruption across the disciplines. Mary Knutsen shows the need for ideology-critique in both philosophy and theology after the event of interruption.

Mary Gerhart argues how the issue of Holocaust literature demands analysis in terms of a genuinely new 'genre' emerging in literary responses to that event.

In the final section, the editors provide some further theological reflections—not by way of 'summary' of the powerful articles themselves but rather by way of an examination of some of the implications of this event of interruption for all Christian theology.

We are especially thankful to the authors of these articles. Each has, on behalf of us all, dared to face the Holocaust, has risked allowing an interruption to all 'thought as usual' which such a risk inevitably demands. They have shown the wider theological community some ways by which we may all begin to address this frightening *tremendum*. As theology enters the concrete history of our times (which these authors dare to address) it is this history that we must all be willing now to face. Sheer linearity, pure continuity and evolutionary historical optimism are finished theologically. History—the real, concrete stuff—is now seen for what it is—interruption.

ELISABETH SCHÜSSLER FIORENZA
DAVID TRACY

PART I

Jewish Reflections

Susan Shapiro

Hearing the Testimony of Radical Negation

THE HOLOCAUST began in 1933, over fifty years ago. The destruction of European Jewry ended in 1945 with the 'liberation' of the concentration camps. However, those boundaries cannot contain the event, the effects of which continues in our lives today.

1. RUPTURE WITHIN LANGUAGE

Not only has the subsequent course of history been shaped by this event, but our assumptions about the world in which we live, about the nature of the human subject and of the Divine, have been thrown into question, even negated. What does it mean to be human in a world that performed and passively witnessed such destruction? And how can we now imagine or conceive of a God who did not save under those circumstances? In what sort of language might we even frame these questions and to whom might we address them? Have not the very coherence of language and the continuity of tradition been broken, shattered by this event?

It is not only the meanings of particular words in particular languages that have been corrupted and, thus, broken by the event. It is the very coherence and meaning of language in general and of God-language in particular that was negated. This rupture within language is the radical negation of our assumptions and conceptions of the human subject that ground the very coherence of language. Furthermore, this rupture within discourse cannot be mended simply by appealing to an undisrupted, ever-available God-language, for our basic conceptions of a Just and Merciful God are themselves thrown into question by the event. Both discourse in general and God-language in particular are thus ruptured, their coherence shattered, their meaningfulness broken.

Three related experiences led to this double rupture of language. The first experience is the Holocaust's victims' pervasive sense of having been abandoned by God. 'Theirs was the kingdom of night. Forgotten by God, forsaken by Him, they lived alone, suffered alone, fought alone.'[1] The second is the purposeful attempt by the Nazis to dehumanise their victims totally before exterminating them.[2] The third experience was the Jews' virtually complete abandonment by the rest of the world to this fate. 'Alone. That is the key word, the haunting theme. Alone with no allies, no friends, totally, desperately alone. . . . The world knew and kept silent. . . . Mankind let them suffer and agonise and perish alone. And yet, and yet, they did not die alone, for something in all of us died with them.'[3] These three dimensions of the experience of the Holocaust ruptured not only the relation between God and humankind necessary for the intelligibility of language about or addressed to God. They ruptured as well those primary social relations and functions, such as friendship, family loyalty, and even the desire to live, that, as *sensus communis*, underlie and found coherent speech itself. Not only did God hang on the gallows with the young boy in *Night*, but the very idea of humanity was incinerated in the Holocaust.[4]

The rupture of language is, thus, not incidental, but central to the radically negative character of the event. The negating character of the event cannot be understood, therefore, as either external or occasional to thought. Rather, it must be recognised as a negation already present in our language, the very instrument of our thought. The breach is not a matter only of institutions that have become systematically distorted and which may, therefore, be subject to critique and then transformed and ethically restored.[5] For language, the very instrument of critique and retrieval, is not simply ready at hand for such a task, but is itself negated and ruptured and in need of critique and recovery.

2. LEARNING TO HEAR THE TESTIMONY OF RADICAL NEGATION

This being the case, we are all, Christian and Jew however differently, implicated within this rupture of and within discourse. It is, thus, this testimony of radical negation that we must learn to hear: Negation in language, negation of language. For what is at stake is our concept of God and our concept of humanness. 'Let us tell tales so as to remember how vulnerable man is when faced with overwhelming evil. Let us tell tales so as not to allow the executioner to have the last word. The last word belongs to the victim. It is up to the witness to capture it, shape it, and then communicate that secret to others.'[6]

'If the Greeks invented tragedy, the Romans the epistle, and the Renaissance the sonnet,' suggests Elie Wiesel, 'our generation invented a new literature, that of testimony.' The drive to testify to the event of the Holocaust was overwhelming. Despite the most horrific of circumstances, writing went on everywhere: in camps, in hiding, while facing certain and impending death. People of every age, including children, in all manner of expression, from diaries and chronicles to poetry and paintings, all felt compelled to record.

> Dear reader, for your sake alone I continue to hang on to my miserable life though it has lost all attraction for me. Time and again I wake up in the middle of the night, moaning pitifully. Phantoms of death haunt me, specters of children, little children. Nothing but children. I sacrificed all those nearest and dearest to me. I myself took them to the place of execution. I built their death chambers for them. And today I am a homeless old man without a roof over my head, without a family, without any next of kin. I talk to myself. I answer my own questions. I am a wanderer. It is with a feeling that all my experiences have become imprinted on my face that I walk. Do I look like a human being? I who saw the doom of three generations must keep on living for the sake of the future. The world must be told of what happened.[7]

The need to communicate, somehow, across the abyss and for the sake of the future, moved people to write about and in every circumstance of horror, despair, and courage. They wrote ceaselessly, passionately, despite the fact that the world was not listening and, for the most part, did not care. Despite this cultivated deafness on the part of most of the world, the victims wrote continuously and obsessively, even, and most often, at great personal risk. This compelling necessity to serve witness to the very horrors of history, this courageous will and risk to communicate, to testify to every detail, to every aspect of the event, itself forms a testimony that demands our attention.

> Rabbis and scholars, merchants and cobblers, anonymous people—all served as historians, as witnesses to history.... To be remembered, that was all they wanted.... Their names, their faces, their songs, their secrets. Their struggle and their death. One as awesome as the other. Not to be forgotten. Hundreds and thousands of men and women joined in conspiracy, often as a self-sacrifice, to enable one messenger to get out and deliver one message, always the same, to the outside world. To bear witness.[8]

Are we, today, listening to this testimony? Have we yet heard its claim? Sadly, tragically for us all, the answer to these questions seem to be clearly, no. Wiesel writes, 'as one who has tried for some twenty-five years to speak on the subject, I feel I must confess to a sense of defeat. The witness was not heard. The world is world . . . our testimony has made no difference.'[9] Consider also the witness of the poet, Nelly Sachs;

> But in the midst of enchantment a
>   voice speaks clearly and amazed:
> World, how can you go on playing
>   your games and cheating time—
> World, the little children were
>   thrown like butterflies, wings
>   beating into the flames—
> And your earth has not been thrown
>   like a rotten apple into the
>   terror-roused abyss—
> And sun and moon have gone on walking—
> Two cross-eyed witnesses who have
>   seen nothing.[10]

If a part of the radically negative character of the event was the apparent abandonment by God and virtually all of the world of the victims of the Holocaust while it was occurring, then our failure today to hear the testimony of those victims is precisely to repeat that radical negativity. As Wiesel writes, 'Anyone who does not actively, constantly engage in remembering and in making others remember is an accomplice of the enemy. Conversely, whoever opposed the enemy must take the side of his victims and communicate their tales, tales of solitude and despair, tales of silence and defiance.[11]

Why is it that this testimony has as yet not been heard, that so very little theological reflection on the event of the Holocaust, especially but not only in the Christian traditions, has been written? One possible reason is the failure on the part of some to recognise that the Holocaust was not a parochial event, but an event that shatters the coherence of all human discourse and of theological language in particular. To hear the claim that the Holocaust makes upon us is not to parochialise our attention. Rather, it is the hearing of its claim in its radical disruption of virtually all of our assumptions about humanity and the Divine. It is, thus, in its radical particularity that the claim of the Holocaust can best be heard. For one cannot hear the claim of suffering in general. In fact, it is always particular individuals and groups who suffer, and it is their distinctive voices that we must both hear and respond to. Rather than deafening one to the voices of the suffering of others, then, the recognition of the uniqueness of the Holocaust radically opens one to the particular and distinctive voices and claims of the suffering of others.

B

3. THE BROKEN LANGUAGE OF THE POETS—A HERMENEUTIC OF RUPTURE

In order better to hear this radically negating claim of the event of the Holocaust, it is especially important to consider the testimony of the poets, for they witness to the shattering of the coherence and the negation of the meaningfulness of language itself. We must listen to them not only in the 'what' of their testimony, but to the witness of their very language. The broken language of these poets of the Holocaust is eloquent testimony to the rupturing effect of that event—rupturing of God-language and of the very syntax of everyday human speech.

The second, related reason for this failure to attend to these voices and their claim is, perhaps, the 'listening' to this testimony from within the inhospitable context of a non-disrupted theology or hermeneutic of tradition. For if our assumptions about the meaning and coherence of language are in principle incapable of disruption or negation, then the testimony of radical negation can in fact never be heard.

How might we, then, better hear this testimony so as to realise that our reflection is implicated within its radically negating claim? We must learn from the hermeneutical struggles of the poets themselves, and we must transform our own interpretative theory and practice into a hermeneutic of rupture. Only then may we truly hear the radical plurality of voices testifying to the event of the Holocaust. Only then may we begin to consider the possibilities of recovery.

Let us first consider the hermeneutical antinomies confronting any poet or novelist attempting to write about or in response to the Holocaust.[12] How can one express or convey the experience of a radically negating event that shatters the very conventions of speech and discourse without employing those conventions and, thereby, domesticating that radical negativity? How can one tell about an event that negates and shatters our assumptions about order (including social relations, conceptions of God, understandings of tradition, history, and time) in discourse, the main function of which is the ordering of human experience? At stake in this *aporia* is an intrinsic betrayal, not related to the content of speech or writing, but rather to the fact that to speak and write at all is necessarily to project a future and, thus, to order and distance oneself from the event by making it past. The other side of the risk, however, is the betrayal implicit in forever keeping silent about the event of the Holocaust, not telling, not witnessing, not testifying. Not to speak about the past is to condemn it to historical forgetfulness, but to speak is to risk immediate subjugation of its radically negative message to an order-making medium, i.e., discourse.

A central hermeneutical problem confronting those attempting to write about the Holocaust (perhaps especially, but not exclusively for those writing in literary or poetic discourse) is, then, how to avoid domesticating the event itself to speech or writing about the event. One hermeneutical strategy employed differently by various poets and novelists was to 'not write with, but against words',[13] so as to testify in this way to the impossibility of fully, actually telling. They thus attempted to write against writing, to write on and against its limits in despairing hope, protest, and prayer. Caught in a world where speech and writing were shattered, that shattering became the poet's very subject matter and instrument.

Speak, you also,
speak as the last,
have your say.

Speak—
But keep yes and no unsplit.
And give your say this meaning:

Give it shade enough,
give it as much
as you know has been dealt out between
Midnight and midday and midnight.

Look around:
... He speaks truly who speaks the shade.[14]

The related hermeneutical strategy of narrating by saying that one cannot fully say is a way of talking about the Holocaust without, thereby, immediately making it simply a subject of, and therefore, subject to, discourse. It is narrated only to the extent that this very unreachability and distance in and from discourse is itself articulated and grasped. As Wiesel has remarked, 'Only one of my books, *Night*, deals directly with the Holocaust; all the others reveal why one cannot speak about it.'[15]

> A matter of words. What kind of words? That, too, became a difficulty the writer had to solve and overcome. Language had been corrupted to the point that it had to be invented anew and purified. This time we wrote not with words, but against words. Often we told less so as to make the truth more credible. Had any one of us told the whole story, he would have been proclaimed mad. Once upon a time the novelist and the poet were in advance of their readers. Not now. Once up a time the artist could foresee the future. Not now. Now he has to remember the past, knowing all the while that what he has to say will never be transmitted. All he can possibly hope to achieve is to communicate the impossibility of communication.[16]

4. REINTERPRETING OUR INTERPRETIVE ASSUMPTIONS

Given the testimony of these hermemeutical struggles with and against language, how might we transform our interpretive theory and practice so as to recognise this radically negating effect of the Holocaust upon language and, relatedly, to represent this belated relationship of language to the event in discourse itself? For how can we attend to the testimony of radical negation if our assumptions about the nature of language, history, and understanding are such that they preclude our even hearing this testimony without, at the outset, subjugating and reducing its claim to those very assumptions about discourse? Attention to the testimony of radical negation is possible, then, only through a systematic reinterpretation of these hermeneutical assumptions in terms of this negation. If critical discourse is to aid in the interpretation of the testimony of radical negation, then its functioning must be reinterpreted as a hermeneutic of rupture.

How might this reinterpretation be effected? We must first recognise that the critical languages with which we approach the interpretation of this testimony themselves partake of the radically negating claim that the discourse they seek to interpret represents. Just as poetic and theological testimony witnesses the rupture of and in language, so the critical language that recognises this testimony of radical negation in the documents it interprets, recognises as well its own, ineluctable implication within that ruptured hermemeutic. In order better to confront the double rupture in language, then, critical discourse must internally negate its own functioning, or more properly, recognise that it has already been so negated by the very event it seeks to interpret.

5. THE EXAMPLE OF GADAMER'S PHILOSOPHIC HERMENEUTICS

Let us consider the example of Hans-Georg Gadamer's philosophical hermeneutics in order better to understand how such an internal negation of critical discourse might be undertaken. Even if one attempted to listen to the testimony of radical negation within the context of Gadamer's hermeneutical theory, there remain powerful pulls toward both the continuity of tradition and the affirmation of meaning within the very *telos* of 'the hermeneutical consciousness' that would ultimately deafen one to the claims of that testimony, unless that *telos* itself were to undergo negation. Consider Gadamer's understanding of 'the hermeneutical consciousness' as evidenced in his essay, 'The Universality of the Hermeneutical Problem':

> The real power of hermeneutical consciousness is our ability to see what is questionable. . . . For we have now reached the fundamental level that we can call . . . the 'linguistic constitution of the world'. It presents itself as the consciousness that is effected by history . . . and that provides an initial schematisation of all our possibilities of knowing . . . [T]he consciousness that is effected by history has its fulfilment in what is linguistic. We can learn from the sensitive student of language that language, in its life and occurence, must not be thought of as merely changing, but rather as something that has a *teleology* operating within it . . . [and this teleology is] the occurrence of the universal . . . that operates constantly in the life of language.[17]

There are three moments in Gadamer's understanding of the hermeneutical consciousness. The first moment is the hermeneutical consicousness as 'the linguistic constitution of the world'. The second moment of the hermeneutical consciousness is that it 'is effected by history'. The third and final moment of the hermeneutical consciousness is that it 'has its fulfilment [teleologically] in what is linguistic'. Although these three moments in principle account for the dynamics of the hermeneutical consicousness as historical, the central, fundamental, and teleological role of the linguistic in that consciousness effectively excludes attention to those historical events that might precisely disrupt its assumptions and claims. For if the very *telos* of the hermeneutical consciousness is itself always assured, then in what sense is it effected by history? It is effected by history in the sense of 'historicity' only, and historicity is itself constituted more by the linguisticality of the hermeneutical consciousness than by actual historical events. The linguistic teleology of the hermeneutical consciousness thus maintains its historicity internally secure from the possible negating effects of actual historical events. The implications of the insularity of such a hermeneutic confronting the event of the Holocaust are serious, inasmuch as it would already reduce historical understanding to a matter of historicity, domesticating at the outset the testimony of radical negation.

If Gadamer's 'hermeneutical consicousness' is to undergo an internal negation so as to be transformed into a hermeneutic of rupture, then a suspension of the insulating functioning of historicity must be undertaken in favour of an attentiveness to the testimony of historical events. The teleology that privileges the order-making functions of language within the hermeneutical consicousness over the claims of actual historical events must be internally negated and suspended if the testimony of radical negation is to be heard. This internal suspension of the *telos* within historicity would entail, for a hermeneutical theory such as Gadamer's, a reinterpretation of the constitutive relations between history and historicity, reversing at least initially their order of priority in the dialectic of tradition. If the hermeneutical consciousness is truly to be effected by history, then the dialectic of tradition must in this way be radicalised, opening itself to the testimony of radically negating events. Otherwise, the hermeneutical consciousness will remain insulated within historicity, but never rise to historicality. Historicity, thus reinterpreted, would then be understood as vulnerable to the claims of historical events, including the testimony of radical negation.

6. RUPTURE AND RETRIEVAL—THE HERMENEUTICS OF TESTIMONY TO TRUTH

Given such a transformation of historicity in terms of an internal negation of its *telos* for the sake of attending to the claims of historical events, how might a hermeneutic be construed or found that situates its own functioning in terms of the radical negativity of the event of the Holocaust, without necessarily succumbing to that negativity? And, conversely, how might a hermeneutic allow for the possibility of recovery without reducing that negativity? For this a hermeneutic of tradition is required that will not at the outset reduce the radical negativity of the event and, yet, will also not foreclose the very possibility of recovery. However, not foreclosing the possibility of recovery must not be construed as a guaranteeing of recovery, for to do so would already reduce the radical negativity of the event. The hermeneutical grounds of the possibility of the recovery of the sacred, therefore, are necessarily tied to a genuine confronting of the radically negative character of the event. Such a recovery of the sacred, I believe, is possible through a dialectical understanding of the hermeneutics of testimony that includes the testimony of radical negation as well as of the possibility of affirmation.

Consider the account in the Babylonian Talmud *Yoma* 68b–69b of the hermeneutics of negation and recovery in the Jewish tradition. In this debate, it becomes evident that, after the destruction of the first Temple, Daniel and Jeremiah[18] deleted the adjectives for God that denoted His might and awfulness. How, the rabbis ask in *Yoma*, were these earlier rabbis (referring here to Daniel and Jeremiah) authorised to do this? Was not such deletion forbidden and blasphemous? The response in *Yoma* is that they were obligated to testify to the truth as they, in their generation, in their historical epoch, saw and experienced it, for God is a living God, and the rabbis must testify to that.[19] But, then, how could later rabbis, for example, Ezra, overturn the ruling of those earlier rabbis by replacing just those previously deleted adjectives? This 'restoration of the crown of the divine attributes to its ancient completeness' is also recounted in *Yoma* 69b.[20] Were they not deleted in testifying to truth? Living well after the destruction of the first Temple, and in the time of the building of the second Temple, perhaps they saw truth differently and were thus able to restore, in testifying to the truth of their historical moment, those formerly deleted adjectives for God's majesty.

However, for us the question arises as to whether this does not speak to us of and in a strange, historically relativistic God-language. And one might answer that the document of *Yoma* itself, in containing these various and seemingly contradictory testimonies, offers us the example and demand of radical testimony in and to one's historical moment for the sake of truth as a hermeneutical and religious necessity. That diverse testimony is contained, but not reconciled, within the classic documents of the tradition itself, serves as both a witness and a challenge. It is a witness to God's presence in history, and a challenge to us to confront that radicality and testify to it in our times.

Notes

1. Elie Wiesel 'The Holocaust as Literary Inspiration' *Dimensions of the Holocuast*, ed. Lacey Baldwin Smith (Evanston 1977), p. 7. See E. Berkouits, *With God in Hell* (New York 1979) for an important and different view of this matter.

2. See Terrence Des Pres *The Survivor: An Anatomy of Life in the Death Camps* (New York 1976).

3. Elie Wiesel, the work cited in note 1, p. 7.

4. Elie Wiesel *Night*, trans. Stella Rodway (New York 1969), p. 76; Elie Wiesel 'A Plea for the Dead' *Legends of Our Time* (New York 1982), p. 190.

5. See Jurgen Habermas's work in critical theory for the term 'systematic distortion'. *Knowledge and Human Interests*, trans. Jeremy J. Shapiro (Boston 1971); *Theory and Practice*, trans. John Viertel (Boston 1973); *Toward a Rational Society*, trans. Jeremy J. Shapiro (Boston 1970); *Legitimation Crisis* trans. Thomas McCarthy (Boston 1975); *Communication and the Evolution of Society*, trans. Thomas McCarthy (Boston 1979).

6. Elie Wiesel 'Art and Culture After the Holocaust' *Auschwitz: Beginning of a New Era?*, ed. Eva Fleischner (New York 1977), p. 403.

7. From an autobiographical account by Yardel Wiernak quoted in Elie Wiesel, the work cited in note 1, p. 14.

8. Elie Wiesel, the work cited in note 1, pp. 11, 16.

9. Elie Wiesel, the work cited in note 6, p. 405.

10. Nelly Sachs 'When in early summer' *The Seeker and Other Poems*, trans. Ruth and Michael mead and Michael Hamburger (New York 1970), p. 147.

11. Elie Wiesel, the work cited in note 1.

12. These antinomies for writing are confronted explicitly, for example, in the works of Paul Celan, Nelly Sachs, and Elie Wiesel.

13. Elie Wiesel, the work cited in note 1, p. 8.

14. Paul Celan 'Speak, You Also' *Paul Celan: Poems*, trans., ed. Michael Hamburger (New York 1980), p. 85.

15. Lily Edelman 'A Conversation with Elie Wiesel' *Responses to Elie Wiesel*, ed. Harry James Cargas (New York 1978), p. 18.

16. Elie Wiesel, the work cited in note 1, p. 8.

17. Hans-Georg Gadamer 'The Universality of the Hermeneutical Problem (1966) *Philosophical Hermeneutics*, trans., ed. David E. Linge (Berkeley 1976), pp. 13–14.

18. In his prayer, *Daniel* 9:4 ff., Daniel omits the word 'mighty', after (according to *Yoma* 69b) saying with respect to the destruction of the first Temple, 'Aliens are enslaving His sons. Where are His mighty deeds?' Jeremiah (according to *Yoma* 69b) said, 'Aliens are destroying (or revel in) His Temple. Where are, then, His awful deeds?' According to *Yoma* 69b, he therefore omitted the attribute of the 'awful', in his prayer, *Jeremiah* 32:17 f. Thus were deleted two of the three divine attributes testified to by Moses in Deuteronomy 10:17, when he said, 'The great God, the mighty, and the awful'.

19. Specifically, *Yoma* states, quoting Rabbi Eleazar, 'Since they knew that the Holy One, blessed be He, insists on truth, they would not ascribe false [things] to Him.'

20. Referring to the account in *Nehemiah* (*Nehemiah* 3:6, 9:4, 32) of Ezra's praise of God, *Yoma* 69b interprets Ezra as either 'magnifying Him by pronouncing His Ineffable Name', ('And Ezra blessed the Lord, the great God', *Neh.* 8:6), or as praising God with all three of His attributes ('The great, the mighty, and the awful God', *Neh.* 9:32). In the later view, Ezra's assembly was referred to as the 'men of the Great Synod . . . [b]ecause they restored the crown of the divine attributes to its ancient completeness'. That is, Ezra restored the praise of the Lord by again praising God with those attributes that Daniel and Jeremiah had omitted.

Arthur Cohen

In our Terrible Age: the *Tremendum* of the Jews

IT IS hard to expect that Christianity, engaged as it is in its own monumental work of redefinition and reconstruction, should take serious time to reflect upon the reentrance of the Jew and Judaism into history. The Jew and Judaism have not been high on the historical agenda of Christianity since long ago it determined to settle its ancient score with the Jewish People by determining its humiliation and supercession. The anti-Judaism of the Church has been so much a part of its own historical breathing that to call it to account, to subject its determinations to critical review, to propose methods of scrutiny that trace to the classical tradition of the gospels and Church Fathers the groundwork of thought and sensibility which would lead nearly two millenia later to the Holocaust, seems as captious and irresponsible as to imply that the Church should cease to breathe. Or to stand the argument on its head, how can Jewish theological observers of the Church suggest that the living Church has been wrong in history, when millenia ago it was already decided that such Jewish observers were bypassed and negated? How can what is 'invalidated' and 'false' survive to speak and pass judgment? And yet it is the case. The Jewish People is, from the view of traditional Christianity, as recusant and unrepentant as the Church is, from the view of Judaism, the preeminent manifestation of its enmity in the world.[1]

But having said all this—describing the general character of the historical scene of classical Western religions—nothing has been said that takes account of our terrible age. The ancient preconditions are alluded, the archtypal deformations adumbrated, but all this would have been true long before the advent of National Socialism and its war against the Jews and the Soviet Union and its war against the Jews. Something has befallen the Jewish People unique in the annals of human brutality: it has been singled out to be exterminated. No modificatory rationalisations, no partitive exclusion of preferential classes or professions, no ideological selectivity was permitted. The *whole* Jewish People— every Jew, every part Jew, every quarter Jew and beyond—was to have been slain. This ideology of extreme 'idealism'—as Adolf Eichmann described his mission in Jerusalem— allowed of no exceptions. The Jew as such, in all Jewish permutations and parts, was to be liquidated. The very extremity and totality of the genocidal mission renders its credibility so extraordinarily *grausam* as to pass understanding. The liquidation of the Jewish People passes understanding and it is the very fact of passing understanding, straining credulity, traducing all canons of conventional historical reason that has provoked my employment of the term *tremendum* to describe it.[2]

It is well known that the term *tremendum* was first used by the great German phenomenologist of the religious, Rudolf Otto (1869–1937) to elicit the aspect of magnificent immensity, tinged with horror, limned with fascination that God's presence presented to Biblical humanity. The God of Scriptures existed and thrived ages before the decretals of reason had begun the consequential work of tying the Lord with cords of deliberation and reflection. That God—the most ancient of all beings—was perceived under aspects so multifarious and complex, so touched with mythic tragedy and pathos, so indited with the lines and markers of raw and naked power and enormity, that such a God could be seen as *tremendum*, magnificent, monstrous, *grausam*, fascinating, awesome, horrifying, in a word, holy. The holy as *tremendum* was precisely that complexity of positive and negative power that befits the master of an ancient universe.

How then speak of the holocaust of the Jews in this century—and the final holocaust of the planet previsaged by the holocaust of the Jews—as *tremendum* if this term is intended to allude to the unfathomable immensity of God? Is *tremendum* then only a metaphor, a literary device, a term whose power rests rather upon its methodological utility than upon its substantial reality? I think not. I take the malign *tremendum* of our century as an absolute index of the limits of human art and freedom, an inversion of the divine, a demonic 'subscendence' countervalent to divine transcendence. If the divine *tremendum* is measured in the distance that describes the abyss between God and man, God's reality and man's theology, God's presence and man's worship, God's futurity and man's historical present, the human *tremendum* is measured in the 'subscendence' that describes the abyss between man's corruption and man's freedom, man's acts and man's ethics, man's ideology and man's faith, man as man does and man as man was created. The God who gave himself in creation and interpreted his nature in revelation is here offset by the extreme man of a rebellious age who has travelled to the limits of his nature and has shown the world how first creation could be maimed in the murder of the Jewish People, and in times to come in the annihilation of the entire human species.

The Jewish People has become in our century the first and unique exemplum of the demonic possibility of a radical human freedom severed from all transcendent controls, indifferent and dehumanising to all churches and their feeble protests, unsusceptible to all challenge and constraint from ethical, much less theological, censure. It does not matter that this modern age still boasts its Church and Synagogue, its observant communicants and believers. It is nonetheless become a world in which there is no God manifest in the councils and deliberation of its leaders. Atheism, not paganism, has ruled the West and the demonic *tremendum* became not only possible, but inevitable. The Jews were the ideal and ordained victim. They, alone of all the peoples of the world, were suited to transcribe the message of a prevailing atheism—an atheism that silenced the Christian faith of pagan principalities and dominions and reduced to temporising, to strategy, to self-interested solutions the conduct of the most powerful of Western churches.

1. THE DEMONIC *TREMENDUM* AS MERELY A WESTERN EPISODE?

We are now in the aftermath of the demonic *tremendum*. Six million Jews are dead. The idealistic adventure was not completed. Millions survived, a State compounded of survivors was founded and to its company other survivors have been gathered, but in the decades that have passed since the skeletons emerged from the death camps, the Christian West has turned its attention to other agendas. Once again, it has become possible for Third World Christians to consider Jews mere prisoners of imperialist capitalism, enemies of the proleteriat and underclassed, conspirators of adventurer nations bent upon the enslavement of poor and groaning societies. Such Third World theologians presume to honour their own constituency by finding once more among the Jews the secret opponent of their ambitions for bread and freedom. The Jews, they aver, are those materialist creatures, unsusceptible of spiritual graces, bonded to a gross and aggrandising regimen, once more spoiling for acquisition. And in the irony of such political rhetoric, the anti-Semitism of the Third World joins with Soviet anti-Semitism, recapitulating the programmatic rhetoric of pre-Fascist anti-Semites, who would make Jews the spawn of capitalism as well as the spawn of communism. Jews have survived such anti-Semitism, not well, but only barely. There is no efficient argument against such venom and hatred. No appeal to Christian virtues nor reminder of the historical consequence of such a malignant teaching suffice.

I propose rather the retreat into theology as the only appropriate and necessary inquiry by means of which to deal with a resurgent anti-Semitism, an anti-Semitism that now treats with increasingly candid and unabashed vigour the *tremendum* of this century as though it were a problem of significance only to Western history. The argument advanced by theologians of the Third World—the emerging nations of Latin and South America, some spokesmen and interpreters of Black African needs and sensibilities, Christian theologians among Middle Eastern and Asian Christian communities—is that the dramas and fatalities of Western Christendom cannot be forced upon the outer Christian communities as if they were paradigmatic. The argument seems to be that the Western experience is peculiarly, idiosyncratically, Western, with little theological reference, meaning, or importance for emerging Christian churches, whose sensibilities, moralities, historical contexts are otherwise determined. It is undoubtedly true that the economic and political realities of nations are dissimilar, shifting as the condition of their people, education, resources, economic distribution, political system varies. But these are social, economic, and political realities. They become religious realities only by extrapolation and by the enforcement of a spiritualising interpretation of their significance. Christian clergy and lay religious may indeed intensify the commitment and relevance of their ministry by transforming the brutal facts of their environment in the light of Christian moral imperatives and eschatological hope, but in doing this they are not effecting a theological transformation of context. They devise no new hermeneutics of retrieving the Christian vocation. At the most, rightly or wrongly, they effect a religious reading of the appalling social and economic conditions to which they are tied in service and work.

What means it then to regard the *tremendum* of the Jews as only a Western episode, an aberration of Western history, no different in structure or kind from any other episodic deformation of Western history, for which—if not Jews—Black Africans, or traduced Muslims, or disadvantaged Latins are asked to pay. The Jews become in such a psychology of displacement merely the old and ancient Blacks and serfs and servile victims of Western imperialism and treachery. In refusing to be in any way enravelled into the predicament and conundrum posed by the holocaust of the Jews, non-Western Christian leaders appear to be saying two things: the extermination of the Jews is a social and political phenomenon, without theological bearing or consequence for Christianity as a whole (since clearly Third World Christians had no hand in it) and also that the extermination of the Jews is a natural, historical event that alludes nothing, signifies nothing, bears nothing from its own time towards the future. Past now forty years, the *tremendum* is to become an epiphenomenon of world history, a concluded historical caesura, aberrational, but without transitiveness or kairotic implication.

Such modes of argument, existentially convenient though they may be, deny critical dimensions of any historical reality—their ontological implication and theological reference. If the *tremendum* of the Jews belongs only to the Western world in general and most particularly to the brutal conflict of Germans and Jews, what portion of history is allowed theological significance? If the first People of God, the inheritors of the ancient covenant, the ethnic descendants of the first Christians—if the history of this People has no relevance for the Christian Church in its fullness then what history at all speaks to Christians?

History is no metaphor and from history there is no exit. In a shrinking world, every portion of the inhabited globe is mutually interactive, one nation's suffering implicated in another nation's prosperity. To imagine that the catastrophes of history somehow belong only to the *dramatis personae* of their enactment is not alone to falsify a reading of history's scale and measure, but to deny to history any portion of God's interest and any generalisation about man's responsibility and guilt. If, indeed, the *tremendum* were only a bother of the Western churches and a calamity to that small remnant of the Jewish People that survived, how shall one call attention to the moral disaster of any other brutality among nations, whether Biafra, Uganda, El Salvador, South Africa, Sri Lanka, Afghanistan? How? By what paradigm shall we speak out against one nations's torment, marshalling conscience against sporadic depredations, selective cruelties, injustice, torture, if the Christian churches (speaking in the qualitative unity of the Holy Spirit) cannot—regardless of from what limb of the Body of Christ they speak—acknowledge that the agony of the Jewish People in this century was a betrayal of Christian faith and promise for which Christians are responsible?

The view of some Christians among the leadership of beleaguered nations of the Third World that the *tremendum* of the Jews does not belong to their history does more than damage the rationale of their own national messianic vision. They purge themselves and their national Christian communities of the link that binds them to the ecumenicity of the universal Church, to the ethical sensorium of the world upon which they rely for succour and surcease, indeed, to the natural charity and affection that promotes support and affection for their cause.

2. THE DIALECTICAL LINK BETWEEN THE COVENANT OF THE JEWS AND THE CHURCH OF CHRIST

Beyond, however, the appeal of moral suasion, to deny the *tremendum* of the Jews a unique place in the history of Christianity in this century is to beat retreat towards precisely the Marcionite deformation of early Christianity that encouraged and elaborated the triumphalism and supercession that ensured the destruction of the Jews.[3] The repudation of Marcion resulted as much from the fact that his doctrine, had it prevailed, would have led in several generations to the wasting of the early Church, due principally to Marcion's requirement that Christians anticipate the *parousia* by ascetic self-denial and total sexual abstinence. That the theological foundation of his social ethics rested upon an exaggerated condemnation of the creator God of Hebrew Scriptures (whom he took to be the preceptor of the dark and unsaved universe), to which was polarised salvation according to Jesus Christ, indeed preserved the dialectic link between the covenant of the Jews and the Church of Christ. But it is not as some interpreters imagine that the excommunication of Marcion was confirmation of the Church's loyalty to Hebrew Scriptures and its revelation. Rather the same set of facts might well be read as the necessary groundwork for sustaining the suppression of the Jewish substratum of Christian faith. Had the God of Israel been expunged from the theological life of the Church, the Jews might well have survived to this day unscathed by the conserved anger of historical Christendom. From the Jewish point of view, the presence and function that Jews have continued to play in the drama of Christian salvation, however softened by the language encouraged by the Second Vatican Council, is one construed and devised for the humiliation of the Jews. The argument can be made (indeed I have made it strenuously elsewhere and it is as yet unrefuted[4]) that the psychological and emotional preconditions to the Marcionist deformation of the Hebrew Bible and its God were anticipated by the gospels, renovated and intensified by Marcion, condemned for reasons that have little to do with Christian sensitivity towards the abashment of the Jews, renewed and strenuously advanced by the most potent anti-Jewish sectors of German Christian Biblical investigation during the last Century, and on their own supplied a strengthened and envigorated strand in the historical matrix that was enacted at Auschwitz.

3. HAS THE ONE AND UNIQUE GOD OF JEWS AND CHRISTIANS PASSED THROUGH 1945 UNSCATHED?

And yet when the argument of historical interpretation is done and Christians and Jews compose themselves again before the one and unique God, is he the same now as he was then, before the *tremendum* of this century? Can we imagine that the God of exquisite perfections—all-knowing, omnipotent, providential, merciful, and just—emerges from the cauldron of our human *tremendum* unrevised? God is of course always in himself; as being he is alwasy unrevised, but God's affectual life on whose attention we depend for revelation and instruction cannot pass through 1945 unscathed and uninspected. If an event of historical caesura, the 'interruption' of which Johann-Baptist Metz speaks, obliges us to rethink our understanding of the nature of God's acts, what is implied is not that God's nature is to be redefined. That nature is always closed to our scrutiny, no differently than the internality of any living being: God's depths are closed and inaccessible. But Judaism understands the nature of God according to the gifts of revelation. The revelation, contained in Scriptures, elaborated and given liturgical voice in the prayer and practice of Jews reflects a sense of divinity which begins instantly—in the very hearing of the assembled multitudes at Sinai—to be interpretation. Nothing that we know of God in our redacted and holy traditions is other than the hearing and rescription of the revealed word. In that revealed word God is nonetheless as deeply concealed as he is disclosed, hidden in the welter of his own actuality, secret in the depths of his being and his intentions for creation. For centuries Judaism strove to make of that body of revelation an *objectivum* and of Jewish tradition its true and trustworthy implication. Although such literal fideism had been sapped by the enlightenment and emancipation, strained by the challenge of modernisation and acculturation (as similar assumption had weakened the theological consensus of Christianity), it was not until the *tremendum* that the edifice of theological monarchism could be seen for what it had become: an archaic structure of interpretation that left the God of history either suspect or irrelevant. The God of ransom and redemption did not ransom and redeem. The repudiating rhetorical assault upon the silent God discloses less about the failure of God than it does about a failed religious language, a language locked into an almost infantile understanding of the divine–human relation.

The task of theology in the aftermath of the *tremendum* is not, it should be underscored, to understand the *tremendum*, to compass and drain it. The *tremendum* remains caesura, a radical interruption and break in the continuous unfolding of the divine–human nexus from creation to redemption. The *tremendum* is an ultimate warning, but not a divine warning. As an ontological gathering of evil, the *tremendum* is an excavation of the abyss beneath the feet of free creatures. It is the warning that mankind gives to itself. It does, however, signal the end of conventional theology of attributes and nomenclatures. By the time of the *tremendum* of this century, the assumptions of classical theology had already passed through the testing fires of radical philosophic criticism that left their validity in doubt, their efficacy depleted. Only by recourse to a precipitous rush to mystery—the biblical mysteries of revelation, phenomenological excursuses on the divine attributes, rhetorical exaltations of awe and wonder—could the postulation of an absolute and monarchic God, whose relations to creation were at best formal and external, be reconciled with the liturgic evocations of a loving, merciful, and just God. The God of classical theism in no way constituted by his creatures or affected by the trials and alarums of created life and its consequential history, had disappeared finally into the folds of mystery, where reason cannot make meaningful the relativity implicit in God's involvement with creation or faith make cogent the remoteness and impassivity that God's absoluteness required.

The *tremendum* forces a resolution of this conflict, not alone as an obligation placed upon reason to give some good account of its occurrence in a universe fashioned by a presumptively omnipotent, omniscient, and providential ruler, but even more as an obligation placed upon our humanity—as creatures without presumptive perfections—to account for the *tremendum* in our world, to justify and redeem, if that is possible, the surpassing suffering of its victims and the unbearable guilt of the history that perpetrated it. This is nothing more nor less than our obligation to account for the reality of God in the aftermath of the *tremendum*. The task entails (beyond the work of constructive theology that makes clear and meaningful the nature of God and his relation to history) the translation of such constructive language into terms that will renew the meaning of creation and authenticate, as more than this century's groans for liberation, the promise of redemption.

Notes

1. In *The Myth of the Judeo-Christian Tradition* (New York, 1970) a central theme of argument is the delineation of Judaeo-Christian theological enmity. The phenomenology of theological enmity that I describe there is intended not in a contentious spirit, but as an indispensable mode of truth-telling.

2. *The Tremendum: A Theological Interpretation of the Holocaust* (New York 1981) is a short book in which, having examined the *tremendum* as an epistemological and phenomenological medium of understanding history, I undertake a reconstruction of classical Jewish theology in the dark light of the *tremendum*.

3. My lecture, 'The Holocaust and Christian Theology: An Interpretation of the Problem', delivered under the auspices of the Historical Society of Israel (Jerusalem 1982) and published in its volume of proceedings, *Judaism and Christianity under the Impact of National Socialism* (1919–1945), 0details this thesis.

4. *Ibid.*

PART II

Christian Reflections

Rebecca Chopp

The Interruption of the Forgotten

1. THE HUMAN SUBJECT WHO SUFFERS HISTORY

TWO IMAGES of the human subject appear in the Holocaust literature: one image is that of the human subject as a 'free', rational agent who controls, dominates and manages history. The other image is that of the one who suffers history in order to survive. In this way traditional views of the human subject as both an actor and as one acted upon are split apart. One human subject is the absolute actor—the Nazi guard with the power of life and death; one is the absolute subject—destruction or survival depends upon a whim beyond any control of the subject. The Western fascination with an anthropology based in history arrives at a tragic pause—on the one hand the human subject cruelly controls history; and on the other hand the human subject completely suffers history.

This Western journey of the human subject in history is also revealed in Latin American liberation theologies. These theologians, attempting to be the voice for the voiceless, also portray an anthropology of an entire class of people without the freedom of control that characterises modernity and without the power and ability to make and interpret history. These people, the poor of the earth, live on the periphery of history. They exist, as Gustavo Gutierrez names them, as 'nonpersons'.[1] The poor are not the autonomous controllers of history, but an entire class who exist in identity and conflict against the persons of history. Latin American liberation theologians and Holocaust authors point to a reality of our world that cannot be denied or forgotten: the reality of massive public events of suffering.

Massive public suffering shatters history in our world. The wanton destruction of millions in our century is hard to forget, and harder still to remember. The cries of the hungry, the shrieks of the political prisoners, and the silent prayers of the oppressed interrupt daily existence. Suffering can no longer be viewed as a purely personal event, asking for interpretation through individual claims to authenticity and meaning. It is now recognised as a public-political event, a collective enterprise interrupting all interpretation but always again demanding transformation and interpretation of the human situation. This historical suffering is a radically unjust suffering. This suffering is not natural—disease, earthquakes, famines,—but it is historical—caused by humanity.[2] If natural suffering raised the question of theodicy because it depended on the assumption of justice and goodness of an existence called God, then this historical suffering raises the question of the subject and the possibility of meaning and value in history.

There are vast differences between liberation theologies and the Holocaust literature, paralleling the differences in the events of Latin American poor and the Holocaust.

Liberation theology arises out of a historical relation of conquest and conversion by Christians and in the context of the Western myth of development. Holocaust literature arises out of the historical persecution of Christians toward Jews and in a specific period of secularisation, industrialisation and the Second World War. Liberation theology speaks out on behalf of a class of people: Holocaust literature witnesses to the destruction/survival of a persecuted race. Holocaust literature reveals the horrors of extermination; liberation theology demonstrates the terrors of mass genocide. These differences can and must not be overlooked. Both liberation theology and Holocaust literature demand that the particularities of each event be taken and accepted in full detail with the greatest impact.

But Holocaust literature and liberation theology share a relationship which is unique among Western religious writings. For Holocaust literature and liberation theology interrupt the activity of and the reflection on the everyday continuation of Christianity. Holocaust literature and liberation theology can be understood together as creating a new theological space, which forces a transfomation of Christianity and a reconceptualisation of Christian theology. Holocaust literature and liberation theology both agree on one foundational assumption; that the challenge to contemporary thought and action is the challenge of massive suffering. Christianity and Christian theology can no longer be content with addressing suffering on an individual level from Christian texts, symbols and traditions but must now criticise, interrupt and transform both action and reflection in light of past, prevailing and potential events of massive suffering. Liberation theology and Holocaust literature interrupt and disrupt Christianity and Christian theology with the question and the quest 'who is this human subject that suffers history?'

That Christianity and Christian theology should be concerned with the concept and history of the human subject is by no means surprising. Both the traditional affirmation of the human creature created in the image of God and the belief in the historical incarnation-resurrection of the Messiah underscores that Christianity is a religion concerned with human life and history. Theologically the doctrines of anthropology and history have always been as important as the doctrines of Christology and God. Calvin was able to explain the uniqueness of the human subject as the reflective relationship with God, that is to be a human subject is to be in a relationship of thanksgiving with God. Or a more modern theologian such as Karl Rahner has been able to affirm theology as anthropology for the human subject is always open to God. The quest for and the question of the human subject in history is fundamentally, to the Christian, a religious task and gift. But Christian theology in its modern form has used history as an occasion to talk of the human subject and the relationship to God. Liberation theology and the Holocaust literature demand that history be received in its full interruptive character. History is not to be understood in terms of process or evolution but in terms of rupture, fragmentation, suffering, totalitarianism, oppression, etc. In this interruption that is history, human subjects must be taken not as abstract subjects but as real victims, and the voices of the tortured, the forgotten, the dead, and the living must be listened to and interpreted in a truly Christian anthropology. Here Christianity must be interrupted and transformed because that for which Christianity exists, the human subject in relation to God, will not be forgotten or denied on the underside of history.

2. CHRISTIANITY AS A PRAXIS OF SOLIDARITY

The event of the Holocaust is not a theoretical question about the meaning of Christianity. Rather it is itself an interruption that brings to the centre and substance of Christianity what has existed at the edges and as the effects—those humans consigned to suffer history. Only within such interruptions exist any possibilities for Christianity, the possibilities of 'a new way' (Gutierrez), a 'Messianic religion' (Johann Baptist Metz), a fundamental transformation of both witness and reflection in the Christian tradition.[3] Christianity must undergo a qualitative change from a mythic and subjective religion to a historical and political religion (Jose Miquez Bonino).[4] This new way, the messianic way of Christianity can only take place as Christianity locates itself with the real human subjects of history, the subjects of concrete effective history. In this location Christian is no longer a mere representation of 'common' human existence at the centre of history but a praxis of solidarity with those who suffer outside the periphery of history. The new location of Christianity in concete human activity is accomplished by the adoption of a radical anthropology stressing both the historicality of the subject and the anticipatory structure of freedom in the subject. This radical anthropology is joined to a philosophy of history concerned with the underside of history. In this way Christianity finds its concern for history and the subject as solidarity with human subjects who suffer history. Christianity is interrupted and transformed in its past, present and future hopes for the human subject in history as a praxis of solidarity with those who suffer.

The human subject with which Christianity is concerned is the actual subject who lives, remembers, hopes and suffers in history. Today this human subject is located in the history of suffering. The image of the 'religious' subject now includes the naked, hungry, dirty, oppressed classes and races on the other side of existence. For it is in suffering that the human subject interrupts the world of technical reason, the market place of exchanges, the discourses on theory to remember the past and to hope for the future. It is in suffering that freedom interrupts as a historical freedom—constituted in and through concrete effective history. Here the anthropocentrism of the Western Enlightened world is intensified and transformed—the human subject as the location of knowledge and freedom is realised only through the constitution of the subject by concrete effective history. This radical anthropology contains three interrelated characteristics: (a) the human subject is fully constituted in a particular historical situation through which memory gives the subject an historical identity, (b) the human subject is an active agent in history, and (c) freedom has an anticipatory structure in the human subject.

The subject is grounded in concrete history and grounded as an active agent whose essential nature is defined by the anticipatory structure of freedom. This anticipatory structure of freedom which recalls the past in the narratives of those who suffer and anticipates the future through Utopia and eschatology becomes the location for a new understanding of transcendence within history itself. Transcendence is located through the anticipatory structure of the human subject as an active agent in history. The memories of the human subject, which today are the memories of the suffering of both the living and the dead, keep alive the historical identity of the subject.[5] The subject who remembers can hope, for the memories have the claim of transcendence, a claim of history yet to be realised, a promise of meaning and truth yet to be fulfilled in the activity of human history.

This human subject is usually not recorded in 'normal' history. This subject records history on scraps of filth buried in mud tombs or makes history in the final screams of death. It is in this history that Christianity finds its new home, in a history that is remembered only by way of a claim forever on the future. The philosophy of history concerns both the understanding of what history is and how it is interpreted. In the interruption of events of massive unjust suffering, history is seen from its underside— history as the history of suffering. Here the subject exists as yet-to-be-realized and criticises that history constituted and written by the victors. The history of suffering includes two important notions for the transformation of Christianity and Christian theology: (a) the dialectic of non-identity in events of radical suffering and in the memory of those events, and (b) the notion of solidarity with those who suffer, both the living and the dead. This philosophy of history is not concerned with 'progress' or 'cycles' but with events of radical unjust suffering—events as diverse as the Holocaust and the Latin American poor. These events cannot be contained in any system of meaning or all embracing theory—the events rupture every interpretation. They are remembered best through the witnesses of narratives. These memories recall and represent the event by revealing the freedom yet to be realised of the human subject. The dialectic of non-identity necessitates the telling and the constant retelling of the memories which reveal and keep alive the precise identity of the human subject as one with the freedom of both a history and a future. Central to the history of suffering is the realisation of the dialectic of non-identity in these events which necessitates the retrieval of witness as a basic category of Christianity. For the dialectic of non-identity—the inability of these events to be contained in theories of interpretation or action and the inability to be corrected or cured in history—is represented best through the witnesses themselves.[6] It is this non-identity character of history as suffering which calls the identification of memory and hope, suffering and freedom in Christianity. Here the dialectic of identification between memory and hope, suffering and freedom can be named by the cross and resurrection of Jesus. This dialectic of identification in the cross and resurrection of Jesus meets with suffering and freedom. Memory and hope in the human experience not to be finalised as an answer but to exist in freedom-to-be realised in history.

The joining of the dialectic of non-identity with the identification of memory and hope, suffering and freedom leads to the second characteristic of the history of suffering as solidarity with those who suffer, both the living and the dead. As a concept of history solidarity underscores the collective nature of the human subject. In events of massive suffering the human subject suffers not as a distinct individual judged by equalitarian Enlightenment standards but as a collective agent belonging to a persecuted race or a marginalised class. Solidarity also broadens the historicality of the human subject beyond any one historical time period. This means, in a positive sense, that the history of freedom is the history of suffering. This also means that solidarity with the dead discounts the totality of any emancipatory project in history. Within the memory of the dead there is no way to atone for events as radical as the Holocaust.

History as interrupted focuses on the telling of the stories of the sufferers, both those destroyed and those who survive. Here history is interpreted to bring forward the dangerous memories which interrupt present historical experience. History is the retelling of the real struggle of the historical subject located in the memories of the suffering. If the radical anthropology turns the autonomous subject of the Enlightenment on its head to constitute the subject through concrete history, then the history of suffering reverses history from the underside, from the history of the other.[7]

The Christian religion has to do with the realisation of the human subject in history. But now the human subject is one who in memory and hope, suffering and freedom, is a real agent in concrete effective history. History is now the history of suffering, history as suffered and witnessed to from the underside, the margins, the death camps, and the torture chambers. Christianity must now stand with those who suffer not because suffering is itself privileged but because within the events of suffering the contemporary historical subject is revealed. Christianity seeks in this way to become an interruption: an interruption of systems which deny suffering or try to find a total cure for the elimination of suffering; an interruption of structures which attempt to control rather than transform history; an interruption of theories which deny memory and narrative as constitutive of the identity of the human subject. Christianity interrupts through the power of memories in the form of narratives to point to the possibilities of transformation. It interrupts not simply as a moment of self-understanding but also as an effective historical force. It is an interruption with a purpose and a content—to recall, to represent and to look forward to the future. Christianity joins the interruption of the suffering in history in its commitment to the historical subject as a subject with a past and a future. It is this human subject in relationship to God which is the content and the goal of Christianity as a praxis of solidarity with those who suffer. It is this human subject in relationship to God who forces the interpretation of Christianity as interruption. But this interruption is, at the same time, a demand for transformation and interpretation.

3. THEOLOGY AS CRITICAL AND POLITICAL

Christianity as a praxis of solidarity with those who suffer demands a new formulation of theology in terms of its nature (theology as political and critical), its method (the political nature of human experience and the deideologisation of the scripture) and its model (theology as transformative).

If Christianity is itself a concrete effective force in history, witnessing to the identification of memory and hope, suffering and freedom as represented in the cross and resurrection of Jesus, then theology is a political activity. It is political because Christianity is fundamentally concerned with the concrete realisation of human freedom in history. The demand to do theology politically is the demand to take account of the historical conditions of all knowledge, to be responsible to the anticipatory structure of human freedom, and to be true to the substance of the theoretical reflection on Christian praxis.

This political activity is a critical activity—it understands the conditions for reflection and action, it criticises present situations and interpretation, and it projects future modes of action and reflection. If theology is done politically, it is done critically for the dual purposes of furthering human enlightenment and emancipation. Christian theology must now attempt to formulate a critical relationship of theory and praxis based on transformation and mediated by practical reason. In this way theology takes account of the mediation of past and present meanings for the human subject but always and only in the context of their future import and thus the future formation of the subject in history.

As theology attempts to be political and critical it emphasises two aspects of its methods—the analysis of human experience as political and the deideologisation of the scriptures. Christian theology analyses human experience as concrete socio-political existence. This existence is collective—the basic characterisation of human life is its corporate nature in various expression through nations, ethnic groups, economic and social systems, religious associations, familial relations, etc. Existence in this collective sense is also historical—groups have historians and exist in history interdependent with other groups. The political as the horizon and context of human existence is again dependent upon the radical anthropology of Christianity stressing the activity of the human subject, the historicality of life, and the anticipatory structure of human subject. Human existence involves facts and values, analysis, critique and projection.

This turn to incorporate the political context of human experience in the method of theology has three special implications: (a) the theologian must constantly be self-critical, (b) there must be a real dialogue with other methods of interpretation and transformation, and (c) method itself takes a political turn to incorporate persuasion and transformation, rhetoric and ethics. The theologian no longer can bracket his/her own situation in the doing of theology but must be interrupted by events such as the Holocaust. The theologian must enter into a real dialogue with disciplines such as political science, economics and anthropology in order to analyse and project future modes of transformation. Theology has no special knowledge to protect and must become an interdisciplinary activity so that the human subject in concrete history may never be forgotten, denied or exterminated. Thus theology adds to its traditional mode of analytics and systematics the modes of rhetoric and ethics, as intrinsic to the imperative as well as the indicative nature of Christian theology.

Along with the political context and horizon of experience, Christian theology seeks to interpret the scriptures. The scriptures contribute to theology a transformative vision. But the scriptures must go through a process of deideologisation in two senses. In the first sense, the text must be interpreted in and through its concrete socio-political context. The importance of the text is understood only through the particularity of the text. In the second sense, deideologisation means the examination of the systematic distortions, or the false consciousness, within the text itself. The project of deideologisation forces us to recognise the distortions of Christianity even within its own classical text. This systematic distortion in the text must be studied, confessed and understood. Christians cannot purge the text, but by remembering the horrors resulting from the text and this suffering in the past and present, Christians may be able to live their faith as a witness that such distortion and persecution shall never again occur. The New Testament prejudice against the Jews must be rendered explicit and accepted as a real distortion within Christianity.

By identifying the change in the nature of theology, and the emphasis in the method of theology, we can summarise a model of this theology. Mindful of the orientation to the future out of the dialectic events of the present and mindful of the identification of the free human subject as represented by the Christian tradition in memory and hope, suffering and freedom, we can call this a model of transformative theology.

Central to this model is the commitment of theology to Christianity as a praxis of solidarity with those who suffer. This praxis takes place in a world marked by events of radical, unjust suffering. The character of these events is a dialectic of non-identity—they cannot be fully understood by theory or corrected by praxis. They shatter any illusion that civilisation is a parade of progress. Events interrupt theories of emancipation and enlightenment to witness to the identity of the human subject in the history of suffering. Indeed, the world in which this theology is born is landscaped by events of massive public suffering which question the existence of a human race that could engineer such events. But here also is the horizon for this theology—that through these events of suffering comes the witness of and to the human subject as a free agent in history, a subject with a history and a future. It is in the radical nature of these events of suffering that the human subject is revealed as one whose identity is to remember, to hope, and in so doing to testify.

The self referent for transformative theology is the historical subject defined by the structure of anticipatory freedom who today is located in the history of suffering. The object referent for transformative theology is the continuing transformation of history by God and humanity. The quest for transformation involves both enlightenment and emancipation as the historical subject concretises his/her identity through the narration of memories and the formation of change represented by Christianity as a praxis of soliarity with those who suffer.

Notes

1. Gustavo Gutierrez 'The Irruption of the Poor and The Christian Communities of the Common People' in *The Challenge of Basic Christian Communities: Papers from the International Ecumenical Congress of Theology* ed. Sergio Torres and John Eagleson, trans. John Drury (Maryknoll 1981), p. 108.

2. Matthew L. Lamb *Solidarity with Victims: Towards a Theology of Social Transformation* (New York 1982), pp. 2–7.

3. Gustavo Gutierrez 'Liberation Praxis and Christian Faith' in *Frontiers of Christian Theology in Latin America* ed. Rosino Gibellini, trans. John Drury (Maryknoll 1979), p. 2; and Johann Baptist Metz *The Emergent Church: The Future of Christianity in a Postbourgeois World* trans. Peter Mann (New York 1981), p. 6.

4. Jose Miguez Bonino 'Five Theses Toward an Understanding of the Theology of Liberation' *The Expository Times* 37 (April 1976), 197–198.

5. Johann Baptist Metz *Glaube in Geschichte und Gessellschaft: Studieren zur einer praktischen Fundamentaltheologie* (Mainz 1977), p. 63.

6. Terrence Des Pres *The Survivor: An Anatomy of Life in the Death Camps* (New York 1976), p. 28.

7. Arthur A. Cohen *The Tremendum: A Theological Interpretation of the Holocaust* (New York 1981), p. 20; and Gustavo Gutierrez *The Power of the Poor in History: Selected Writings* trans. Robert R. Barr (Maryknoll 1983), p. 201.

Johann-Baptist Metz

Facing the Jews. Christian Theology after Auschwitz

I EXPRESSED myself before about the relationship between Christians and Jews after Auschwitz.[1] In doing so I used a high-pitched tone which was too radical for many Christian ears. At this time I cannot simply repeat what I said before; but neither do I want to recant anything. I shall try to elaborate on it.

Sören Kierkegaard: In order to experience and understand what it means to be a Christian, it is always necessary to recognise a definite historical situation. I start with the idea that Kierkegaard is right (without being able to explain this in detail at this time). The situation without the recognition of which Christian theology does not know whereof it speaks, is for us in this country first of all 'after Auschwitz'. I would like to present my thoughts in a few theses.

> *First thesis:* Christian theology after Auschwitz must—at long last—be guided by the insight that Christians can form and sufficiently understand their identity only in the face of the Jews.

This brief statement is extraordinarily well backed up in the Bible—Romans 9–11—and by the echo on the part of present-day Christian theologians (during the Nazi period there were Bonhœffer and Barth, afterwards theologians such as Eichholz, Iwand and the grouping around the Rhenish Synod, and on the Catholic side theologians such as Thomas, Mussner, Zenger as exegetes), and by the echo in recent Church documents.

Just the same, it seems to me that the importance of the statement is not yet completely recognised in its consequences by Christian theology. First I want to call attention to the fact that the thesis does not say that our Christian identity has to be established and ascertained in the face 'of Judaism', but in the face of 'the Jews'. I utter this differentiation intentionally. We must finally be on our guard against all subject-less terminology, but most of all in the case of the Jews. 'Judaism' as such has no face and no eyes which can be remembered. 'Judaism' can again and again be interpreted down and objectified by 'Christianity'—interpreted down and objectified as an outdated precursor of the history of Christianity. Yes, it can be objectified, so that present-day Jews need not be seen either as partners nor even (only) as opponents. After all, even opponents have a face! For the sake of Auschwitz they have to be seen—the destroyed faces, the burned eyes, of whom we

26

can only tell, which we can only remember, but which cannot be reconstructed in systemic concepts.

This short linguistic observation with regard to our theological language contains already a decisive demand. This demand is directed against the use of system concepts and aims at the decisive use of subject concepts in the realm of theology. This demand for a subject-based rather than a system-based kind of Christian theological concern is not the expression of a privatistic or individualistic form of theological consciousness. It is the natural consequence of 'historical consciousness' in the field of theology—demanded of us, expected of us and granted to use in the face of Auschwitz. Even this first demand may show that here, with the view toward Auschwitz, it is not a matter of a revision of Christian theology with regard to Judaism, but a matter of the revision of Christian theology itself.

In order to obey the historical demand for a transition from system concepts to subject concepts, Christians and especially Christian theologians must learn to say 'I' in a new manner and thus can no longer disguise their historical lack of sensitivity with an objective system language. To say 'I' as a Christian theologian in the face of Auschwitz: this does not mean a stylisation of theological individuality, but a sensitivisation for a concrete crisis situation such as the one which confronts present-day Christian theology and in the midst of which it wants to find the truth of the Gospel and testify for it—after Auschwitz. This kind of saying 'I' must be learned categorically; it is by no means subjectivistic or uncritical, and also not unpolitical. As far as I am concerned, it is the teaching aim of Christian theology after Auschwitz. After all, the time of situationless and subjectless systems—as privileged locations of theological truths—is no longer with us, at least not since the catastrophe of Auschwitz, which no one may ignore without being a cynic, and which no one should be permitted to forget within an objective sense system.

I would like to explain briefly in three areas what this means for me—to say 'I' in the face of the Jews, in the face of the catastrophe of Auschwitz. Let me *first* talk of the milieu out of which I came: I am a boy from the country, from an arch-Catholic Bavarian small town. Jews were actually not seen in this town; even after the war they remained mere shadows or cliches; our views of how Jews looked came from—Oberammergau. The catastrophe of Auschwitz, which finally became the catastrophe of Christianity, did not enter our consciousness; nothing was heard about it, although my home town was located barely 50 km from that concentration camp in which Dietrich Bonhœffer was killed—not least because of his attitude toward the Jews. The Church milieu of the little town from which I come, and also the milieu of the neighbouring town where I attended high school, never called my attention to Auschwitz.

To learn to say 'I' in the face of the catastrophe of Auschwitz is *secondly* above all a job for *theology* itself. I had the good fortune to learn that Catholic theology which in my eyes was the best of that time, and to it I owe everything that I can do theologically myself. I mean the theology taught by Karl Rahner. To be sure, gradually, much too gradually, it dawned on me that even in this theology Auschwitz was not mentioned. Thus, in confrontation with this catastrophe, I began to ask critical questions and to look for additional viewpoints of theological identity. Were we still caught in a kind of historical idealism? Did the logos of Christian theology still have much too high a content of apathy? Too much fortitude against the abysses of historic catastrophes? This was perhaps the reason why (especially immediately after the war) we talked so much about the 'historicity' of faith and theology in order to cover up the real contradictions of historical experience through this formalism. Wasn't there a too-demanding, supposedly christologically motivated historical triumphalism at work, an overly-strong sense optimism against history, which blinded us against the real threats confronting our Christian hope? Didn't we know, ahead of any Christian practice, too much about the sense of history, which makes every catastrophe merely appear like the echo of a departing thunderstorm? It seems that we did not know that for the understanding of our own history and our own promises we had to depend on a non-Christian partner, on our victims, in short on the Jews of Auschwitz.

Exactly in looking at Auschwitz it became clear to me that an adequate separation between systematic theology and historical theology, between truth and history, is not possible—even with the best of wills. And this is true for both—the systematic theologians and the historical theologians—each in their own way. Historical theologians, too, cannot simply and without problems submit to a scientific knowledge, which defines historical knowledge against memory knowledge. The Auschwitz catastrophe cannot simply be historically reconstructed, it must be remembered practically. For this reason our historical theologians must reintroduce the 'struggle for remembrance', the struggle for the subject-centred memory knowledge, into the general understanding of history. Historical theologians most of all, (with the accent on 'theologians') must try to see the scenario of history with the eyes of the victims; they must know that they are engaged by society as attorneys for the dead (as formulated in a similar way by H. Oberman), as intermediaries between democracy and tradition, by interpreting democracy not only as space, but also as time—in other words that they will try to expand democracy backwards and thus try to gain the votes of the dead (as similarly postulated by G. K. Chesterton). How would the history of our recent past look then? Historical consciousness and historical conscience are not tested mainly in looking at successes and victories, but in the occupation with defeats and catastrophes. In them we meet what history draws from all 'evolutionistic' explanations taken from nature: the discontinuity: the pain of negativity, the sufferings; and in all of them: the catastrophe, the practical challenge to one's own hope.

There is no truth for me which I could defend with my back turned toward Auschwitz. There is no sense for me which I could save with my back turned toward Auschwitz. And for me there is no God to whom I could pray with my back turned toward Auschwitz. When that became clear to me, I tried, no longer to engage in theology with my back turned to the invisible, or forcefully made-invisible, sufferings in the world; neither with my back toward the Holocaust nor with my back turned to the speechless sufferings of the poor and oppressed in the world. This probably was the starting point toward the construction of a so-called political theology.

Third: Let me also briefly refer to the saying of 'I' in the face of the Jews by pointing to *religion* and religious practice. In religious practice, such as practised by me (as a boy during the Nazi period) the Jews did not appear. With our back toward Auschwitz we prayed and celebrated our liturgy. Only later I began to ask myself what kind of a religion it is that can be practised unmoved by such a catastrophe. This was one of the reasons why I began to speak of Christianity critically as a 'bourgeois religion'. (Much could be said about this also. But I will continue with my next thesis.)

> *Second thesis:* Because of Auschwitz the statement 'Christians can only form and appropriately understand their identity in the face of the Jews' has been sharpened as follows: 'Christians can protect their identity only in front of and together with the history of the beliefs of the Jews.'

It is the task of a Christian theology after Auschwitz to make this situation publicly clear. Let us look for a moment at the renewal of the relationship between Christians and Jews in the post-war period. We can observe *different phases and dimensions of this renewal.* First the phase of a diffuse affection, which for its part is not very stable or safe from crises and can easily disappear (and which is hardly aware of the fact that such a diffuse philosemitism can easily be and remain a masked form of anti-Semitism). Next the phase of the theological discussion of the transition 'from mission to dialogue'. And finally the beginnings of a conscious theological rethinking, the development of a Christian theology of Judaism post Christum, with a recognition of the lasting messianic dignity of Israel, the 'root' significance of Israel for the Church (as was already claimed by Bonhœffer and Barth). The fourth phase would finally be the following: the recognition on the part of Christians of their concrete faith-historical dependence on the Jews, i.e. in line with the thesis that Christians even in their own identity can no longer define themselves without the Jews.

Here 'Auschwitz as an end' is taken seriously theologically, but not as an end for a definite phase of Jewish history, but as an end of that kind of Christianity which refuses to form its identity in the face of and together with the Jews. In the final analysis, to say it once more—with a view toward Auschwitz—it is not only a matter of revising Christian theology with regard to Judaism, but a matter of revising Christian theology altogether. Of this I talked briefly in an earlier paper, and from this paper I repeat once more: What I personally mean by calling Auschwitz the end and turnaround for us Christians, I can make clearer by referring to a conversation. In 1967 there occurred a discussion in Münster between the Czech philosopher Milan Machoveć, Karl Rahner and myself. Toward the end of the conversation Machoveć referred to Adorno's statement: 'After Auschwitz there won't be any poems any more.' Then he asked me whether after Auschwitz there could still be prayers on the part of us Christians. I gave the same answer that I would give today: 'We can pray after Auschwitz, because there were prayers in Auschwitz.' We Christians can no longer go back behind Auschwitz, but neither can we go beyond Auschwitz except together with the victims of Auschwitz. This, in my eyes, is the root of Jewish-Christian ecumenism. The turnaround in the relationship between Jews and Christians corresponds to the radicality of the end brought about by Auschwitz. Only if we face it resolutely will we know what the 'new' relationship between Jews and Christians really is or at any rate could be.

This connection I would like to make clearer and explain more fully by discussing the so-called *theodicy question in the face of Auschwitz*, i.e. the 'god question' in the face of these fearful sufferings. I would like to discuss what is meant by this for us Christians and for our understanding of ourselves, by reference to a book which has become very famous, because it is a very unique work—I refer to Elie Wiesel's book *Night*. The text has already become prototypical; many Christian theologians are quoting from it. For this reason I can most easily explain my intentions with its help. 'The camp commanders refused to serve as hangmen. Three SS men took over the job. Three necks were put into three nooses within a short moment. "Long live freedom!", shouted the grown-ups. But the child said nothing. "Where is God? Where is he?", said someone behind me. The three chairs were tipping over . . . We marched past . . . The two men were no longer alive . . . but the third rope was still moving . . . the child was lighter and was still living . . . Behind me I heard the same man ask: "Where is God now?" And behind me I heard an answering voice: "Where is he? Here he is—he hangs on the gallows." In this night the soup had the taste of corpses.'

I would like to make comments to this text only in one regard. *Who* really has the right to give the answer to the God-question—'Where is God? Here he is—he hangs on the gallows'? Who, if anyone at all, has the right to give it? As far as I am concerned, only the Jew threatened by death with all the children in Auschwitz has the right to say it—only he alone. There is no other 'identification' of God—neither as sublime as for instance in J. Moltmann nor as reserved and modest as in the case of D. Sölle—here, as far as I am concerned, no Christian-theological identification of God is possible. If at all, this can be done only by the Jew imprisoned together with his God in the abyss—it can be done only by him who himself finds himself in that hell 'where God and human kind full of terror look into each other's eyes' (Elie Wiesel). Only he, I think, can alone speak of a 'God on the gallows', not we Christians outside of Auschwitz who sent the Jew into such a situation of despair or at least left him in it. Here, for me, there is no 'sense', to which we could testify without the Jew. Without the Jews in the hell of Auschwitz, we are condemned to Non-sense, to God-lessness.

Let us not say: After all there are for us Christians other God-experiences beside Auschwitz. That's true! But if there is no God for us in Auschwitz, how can there be a God anywhere else? Don't tell me that such an idea violates the core of Christian self-understanding, according to which the nearness of God is definitely guaranteed through Jesus Christ. There still is the question what kind of Christianity is entitled to this guarantee. Perhaps that Christianity identifying itself as anti-judaistic, which belongs to the historical roots of Auschwitz, or a Christianity which knows that it can form and understand its own identity only in the face of the Jewish history of suffering?

That in the God-question itself we should be dependent on the testimony of the Jewish history of sufferings: this seems to be going too far for many Christians. For me, however, the recognition of this quasi-salvation historical dependence is the very criterion as to whether we Christians are ready really to acknowledge the catastrophe of Auschwitz as a catastrophe and whether we are really ready to take it seriously theologically as the challenge which we cite so frequently moralistically. I repeat that with a view toward Auschwitz it is not merely a matter of revising Christian theology with regard to Judaism, but a matter of revising Christian theology altogether.

Of course there are enough *symptoms* showing that we want to keep this radical challenge through Auschwitz far away from us. There is, *for instance*, the attempt to eliminate the Holocaust from specifically Christian causality altogether. It is considered a purely National-Socialist crime, which, as is stressed in the Bonn Paper, was 'as much anti-Jewish as anti-Christian'; or one sees this catastrophe only as a result of the 'German Spirit' (which idea is opposed by H. Obermann in his latest book). Or, *secondly*, one has resort to quick reinterpretations of the holocaust catastrophe, that is, Auschwitz is made into a type or symbol for all kinds of threatening or possible catastrophes in the world, and forgets that the over-all validity of the Jewish tragedy and of Holocaust is found exactly in its non-transferability, in its uniqueness and its incomparability. Just as the Church once upon a time thought, by means of a dangerous substitution theory, that it could inherit or ignore the historical fate of Israel ('The church as the real Israel'), so we find today profane substitution theories for Auschwitz which run the danger of making the catastrophe of Auschwitz appear unimportant by simply transferring it to other situations of suffering. A *third* form of removing the tension in the Christian God-Question posed by Auschwitz is found in the attempt to connect the name of Auschwitz with the tragedy of Jews 'and Christian'. It is certainly true that there were also Christians, even heroic Christians in Auschwitz, but we must with all our determination stress the fact that this name stands for the fearful tragedy of the Jewish people. We must do this for the sake also of these Christian martyrs, who after all often were sent to Auschwitz because of their solidarity with the Jews. I tried to use these arguments during the joint Synod of the dioceses in the Federal Republic of Germany (1975) when I had to present the paper 'Our Hope' which had been pre-formulated by me (within the responsible commission). My arguments were not fully accepted (the text speaks of 'Jews and Christians'), but at any rate this passage of an official synod document contains the most advanced statement concerning the new relationship between Christians and Jews in the face of Auschwitz. In it we read in so many words: 'We in Germany of all places must not deny or make appear harmless the salvific connection between God's people of the old and the new covenant which had already been seen and confessed by Paul the Apostle. Because in this sense, too, we in our country have become debtors of the Jewish people. After all, the credibility of our talk of the "God of Hope" in the face of a hopeless error such as Auschwitz, depends above all on the fact that there were innumerable people, both Christians and Jews, who in this kind of hell again and again called on God and prayed to him.'

Fourth, very briefly, I would also like to call attention to the 'handoffering' of the Rhenish synod which courageously enters upon the theodicy problem in the face of Auschwitz. To be sure it seems to me a case of false modesty when it is recommended that the God-question should 'be kept open', which modesty hides the dependence in the treatment of the God-question after Auschwitz on the Jewish history of sufferings. I hope I need not mention that I do not expect a speculative reply to the theodicy question. My problem is to discover whether and how we Christians can and may speak of 'God after Auschwitz' in a credible constellation.

However, I would not want to overlook the fact that Auschwitz is not only a question of theodicy, but certainly also a very dramatic question of *anthropodicy* to which attention has frequently been called. It is the question of the justification of *humankind* in the face of the sufferings at Auschwitz. In this sense the question asked by Elie Wiesel could also be formulated with a view toward anthropodicy as follows: 'Where was humankind in Auschwitz'? Many survivors went to pieces exactly because this question could not be answered because they could not longer believe in humankind. How can you continue to live among men if in Auschwitz you had to find out what they are able to do? As you know this question opens the tragedy of Auschwitz from an entirely different point of view, which I cannot discuss here. I shall go on to the next thesis.

Third Thesis: Christian theology after Auschwitz must stress anew the Jewish dimension in Chrsitian beliefs and must overcome the forced blocking-out of the Jewish heritage within Christianity.

This thesis does not merely want to bring back into the memory of Christian theology the Jewish existence of Christ himself. It aims at the Jewish-originated form of the Christian faith. To say it once more: the problem, with a view toward Auschwitz, is not merely a revision of the Christian theology of Judaism, but of a revision of Christian theology altogether. The thesis speaks of a 'mode of believing'. This means that I adopt a statement by Martin Buber ('Two modes of believing'), without, however, simply taking over the differences outlined by him. 'Modes of believing' here are intended to characterise the tying together of faith content and faith exercise, of subject and object, of faith theory and faith practice, of theory and practice. I assume—in contrast to Buber—that there is not only a specifically Jewish Old-Testament manner of belief and a specificially Christian New-Testament manner of belief, but that in the traditions of the New Testament, differing modes of believing are present. Thus it is undoubtedly possible—although I am not able at this time to enter upon this problem in detail—to speak of a pronounced synoptic mode of believing in contrast to a pronounced Pauline mode of believing, but without the two manners being exclusive of each other. Obviously the synoptic manner of believing is influenced more strongly and more lastingly by the Jewish Old-Testamentary manner of believing. But just because this synoptic manner of believing stepped into the background as against the Pauline manner of believing in the course of Christian history—just because of this it must again be remembered and again identified as a 'Christian mode of believing'. This Jewish-formed mode of believing belongs in the basic situation of the Christian faith. It was not taken from the Old Testament, but exactly from the New Testament itself.

Faith as a trusting yielding to the will of God means here above all a being-on-the-road, a being-underway, even a being-homeless, in brief: discipleship. Christ is truth and way.

Every attempt to know him, to understand him, is always a going, a following. Only if they follow him do Christians know with whom they are associated and who saves them. This kind of christology is not primarily formed in a subjectless concept and system, but in discipleship stories. This kind of Christology is not primarily formed in a subjectless concept and system, but in discipleship stories. This kind of Christology does not bear casually, but fundamentally narrative features. This Christology of discipleship stands against a Christianity which interprets itself as a bourgeois religion; it opposes the idea that Christianity is totally at home in the bourgeois world. This Christology of discipleship also stands against that kind of Christianity which considers itself as a kind of religion of victors—with a surplus of answers and a corresponding lack of passionate questions in the being-on-the-way. This christology of discipleship makes it clear that Christianity, too, ahead of all system knowledge contains a narrative and remembrance knowledge. Narration and remembrance correspond cognitively to a belief which understands itself as a going, as a being-underway, as a constitutional form of homelessness. I learned the significance of 'remembrance' and 'narration', if I understand it at all, mainly from Jews, believing or unbelieving Jews, not only from G. Scholem, but also from W. Benjamin; not only from M. Buber, but also from E. Bloch; not only from F. Rosenzweig, but also from E. Fromm; not only from N. Sachs, but also from Fr. Kafka. But Christianity, too, is in its roots a community of remembrance and narration. And it is true that its centre is not an entertaining, but on the contrary a dangerous story, and it invites not merely to reflection, but also to discipleship.

It is the Jewish-formed synoptic manner of believing which calls our attention to the fact that the Christian belief is a sensuous happening, a happening of the senses which cannot simply be spiritualised into purely a faith of attitude. Haven't we been confronted for a long time by the danger of total spiritualisation and inferiorisation of evangelical contents and imperatives? Hasn't discipleship become for us too much a matter of disposition for discipleship, love a matter of disposition for love, suffering a matter of disposition for suffering, exile a matter of disposition for exile, persecution a matter of disposition for persecution? How would it otherwise be possible that Christian theologians, for example, can say that we, the Christians, are the 'real' religion of exile, the 'real' religion of the Diaspora, of the painful dispersion in the world. Can such a statement be defended in the face of Jewish experience through the centuries? Kafka has described it in his 'Letters to Milena': 'This means, to express it in an exaggerated manner, that not a single second of rest is left to me, nothing is given to me, everything must be acquired, not only the present and the future, but also the past—something which perhaps every human being has been given, even this must be acquired, which is perhaps the hardest labour. If the earth turns towards the right—I don't know whether it does so—I would have to turn left in order to catch up with the past . . . It is as though before every single stroll a person does not only have to wash and to comb himself, etc., which is a good deal of labour in itself, but— because before every stroll all that is necessary is again and again missing—the stroller would also have to sew clothing, make boots, manufacture the hat, and cut the walking stick etc. Of course all this cannot be done well, perhaps it will last through a couple of alleys . . . And finally, in the Eisengasse, he may well meet a crowd of people hunting Jews.'

Still other Jewish-influenced features of a Christian manner of believing, as found above all in the synoptic gospels, must be recalled and brought back to life, for instance faith as resistance willing to suffer against powerful social prejudices, and this in the face of a history of Christianity which as against political powers shows much too little history of resistance 'in the name of God'. Rather this history was too much a history of adaptation and obedience. Faith should also not hide its own messianic weakness and should know— unlike an expectation-less hope—that it is not already from the start armed against all historical disappointments—faith for which exactly the God Jesus Christ remains the *other one*, the uncomprehended, even the dangerous God, etc. Didn't we Christians leave behind us too fast the Jewish God-Mystic and prayer piety, even though we know them from the God-experience of Jesus in the synoptic gospels?

Fourth thesis: Christian theology after Auschwitz must regain the biblical-messianic concepts for its ecumenical endeavours.

Exactly in this situation 'after Auschwitz' it should become clear to us that we can only promote unity among the Christians if in this ecumenical endeavour we do not forget that partner who belongs in the eschatological situation of Christians—the Jewish partner. In this sense Karl Barth could remind us that there really exists only one great ecumenical task—our Christian relationship with the Jews. In conclusion I would like to add only one more thought. Only if we Christians do not push aside this messianic perspective of the ecumenical movement, in other words if we develop the thought of Christian unity only with an eye on the Jewish partner—only then will it be possible for us to contribute productively to an ecumenism of the great religions as a whole—at least to a coalition of religions to resist the apotheosis of hatred and banality in the world. Here I am thinking above all of our attitude toward the religion of *Islam*. To me it seems that a direct approach of Christians to Islam, so-to-speak by passing Judaism, seems not possible either theologically or culture-historically. After all is said and done, we must not forget one thing: the Jewish religion, despised and persecuted, is and remains the root religion for both Christianity and Islam. Auschwitz, therefore, is and remains a hateful attack against the roots of our common religious history. Some of you may have missed a critical statement on the present politics of the State of Israel.

But: we as Germans: we have no choice in this matter.

Notes

1. See the article 'Christians and Jews after Auschwitz' appearing in my volume entitled *Beyond Civic Religion* (Mainz-Munich 1980), 29–50 ('Christen und Juden nach Auschwitz' in *Jenseits bürgerlicher Religion*, by J. B. Metz (Mainz-München 1980) pp. 29–50).

Gregory Baum

The Holocaust and Political Theology

BEFORE, DURING and after the Holocaust the Christian world remained silent. There were a few courageous men and women who spoke up or who acted. God was not totally left without witnesses.

1. BELATED REPENTANCE

After the War several Christians, Protestant and Catholic, began to ask themselves whether and to what extent the Christian tradition itself had contributed to the genocidal mass murder. They recognised of course that Nazism was anti-Christian and that Nazi racism rejecting everything Jewish also repudiated Jesus and the New Testament, but they believed that the anti-Jewish teaching and symbols present in the Christian tradition had created a cultural world in which the anti-Semitic language and sentiment of the Nazis were able to spread so rapidly and where people had a vague feeling that the destruction coming upon the Jews was a providential punishment. Of great importance was the book *Jésus et Israel* (1948) by the French historian Jules Isaac, himself a Jew, which demonstrated that contempt for Jews and the denigration of Jewish religion were elements of Christian preaching almost from the beginning. While at first only a few Christians had the moral courage to study this material and confront the issue, their number grew; they organised, published their own reviews, established research centres, and eventually succeeded in influencing the leadership of the churches.

During the sixties, church councils and church boards, Protestant and Catholic, with varying degrees of honesty and repentance, made important public declarations that expressed their great sorrow over the giant evil inflicted upon the Jews. They repented of their silence, repudiated the anti-Jewish elements of Christian teaching, gave up proselytism in regard to Jews, and demanded instead solidarity with the Jewish people. In many churches these declarations led to the re-writing of catechisms, religious education material, liturgical texts, and theological treatises. Many churches, especially in North America, gave public expression to their solidarity with the State of Israel.

As Christians in ever greater number wrestled against the distortions in their own tradition, they discovered to their dismay how deeply the negation of Jewish existence was inscribed in the presentation of the Christian message. The Christian way was always presented as the supersession of the religion of Israel: with Jesus Christ, Judaism had lost its validity. Anti-Judaism, as Rosemary Ruether has formulated it, was here 'the left hand of Christology'.[1] Is it possible to proclaim the Christian Gospel in fidelity to Scripture in a manner that respects and honours Jewish religion? Taking seriously the Holocaust meant for some theologians the re-thinking of Christology. Jesus Christ became for them the Great Protector of humans, who stood against all the forces of death.

The Holocaust remains forever a principle of discontinuity for the Christian Church. No amount of rethinking and reformulating the Christian message and no amount of dialogue and cooperation with Jews will ever allow the Church to be reconciled with its past. As part of Western civilisation, the Church stands convicted by its silence. Holocaust is unique for Christians. The silence of the world may simply have been indifference to the suffering of others; the silence of the churches was more than indifference. It expressed a vaguely religious sense that the Jews were not our brothers and sisters, they represented something antithetical to the Christian vision of society, they bore the mark of Cain on their foreheads, and they were now visited by a mysterious providential act. Confronting the Holocaust now Christians discover that there are no innocent bystanders. Confrontation with the Holocaust provokes discontinuity and restlessness in the Church. Christians can no longer be silent, even if their speaking reveals the complicity of their own Church. Christians must forever examine the ideological distortion of their own religious tradition.

Because of this double challenge, 'Speak out against social evil', and 'Examine your own complicity in this social evil', the belated Christian response to the Holocaust affects the Church not only in its relation to Jews but more universally in its relationship to the world.

The silence of Pope Pius XII has become the symbol of the Church's guilt. Hochhut's play *The Deputy* has given this symbol great cultural power. Since then the Church has begun to speak out on social evil. At one time, the Catholic Church regarded itself as protector of the inherited Christian civilisation. It spoke out on political matters only when its own institutional interests were at stake, or when modern, liberal society violated traditional ethical norms related, for the most part, to procreation and family life. The Church observed a respectful silence in regard to the conflicts between nations: at best, it offered diplomatic channels for peaceful reconciliation. Pius XII remained silent when Hitler invaded Poland, even though Poland was an ancient Catholic land. The German bishops also remained silent. The silence of Pope and bishops before the persecution and later the mass murder of the Jews is better known.

2. PUBLIC WITNESS TO JUSTICE

Since the Second World War, the Churches, including the Catholic Church, have begun to speak out against social evil. They have often done this out of a spirit of repentance over their silence during the mass murder of the Jews. In response to the Holocaust bishops have become spokesmen for peace, justice and human rights.

The Pastoral Letter on War and Peace (May 1983) published by the American bishops is, in my opinion, historically incomprehensible without taking into consideration the Holocaust and the Church's silence during the Second World War. The American bishops at this time believe that their own country is moving in the direction of mass destruction, the dimensions of which stagger the imagination. The world is driven toward self-destruction through the logic of the nuclear arms race—a demonic evil. Traditional just war theories no longer apply to nuclear weapons. Because of their enormous power and the uncontrolled nature of their destruction, they exterminate whole populations. They make total war against innocent people. There can be no moral justifiction for nuclear bombing. Americans must not forget, the bishops argue, that they were the first country to produce the atomic bomb and the only country ever to drop it. They now ask the Catholic people to influence public opinion so that it becomes possible 'for our country to express profound sorrow over the atomic bombing in 1945'. 'Without this sorrow', the bishops add, 'there is no possibility of finding a way to repudiate the future use of nuclear weapons'.[2] It is hard to find parallels in church history for a declaration made by the bishops of a superpower that offers resistance to the crimes of empire.

Since the Holocaust the churches have begun to examine their own complicity in social evil. In theology this is known as 'ideology critique'. The German and North American theologians who, under the name of 'political theology', have engaged in ideology critique as an indispensable step in the clarification of the Christian message for our age, have all been profoundly affected by the encounter with the Holocaust. This is true especially of the German theologians Metz,[3] Moltmann,[4] and Soelle.[5] It is also true of North American political theologians, such as Robert McAfee Brown,[6] Francis Fiorenza,[7] Matthew Lamb,[8] and Rosemary Ruether.[9] It is no coincidence that the term 'ideology critique' is derived from the Critical Theory of the Frankfurt School, which engaged in an extended critique of anti-Semitism before the War and which, especially in the writings of Adorno and Horkheimer,[10] dared to face the judgment on civilisation implicit in the Holocaust. It is in obedience to the challenge of the Holocaust that Christian thinkers, and in some cases even Christian churches, have taken sides with the victims of society and truthfully examined the hidden complicity of Christianity with the forces of oppression.

3. LIBERATION THEOLOGY

In this context it is necessary to mention another historical event, one of an altogether different nature, that also had a profound effect on the self-understanding of the Christian Church. It also generated the twofold challenge, 'Speak out against social evil', and 'Examine your own complicity in this social evil'. The event I am referring to is the breakdown of Western empire. In the past the churches had legitimated the rule of Western empires over other peoples and continents, first when it took place through military conquest and commercial exploitation and later when it was exercised through the extension of the Western economic system. The Church accompanied the colonial expansion of Western powers to extend its mission and plant Christian communities in the distant lands. Now it is precisely these churches of colonial origin that accuse of complicity the churches identified with empire. The former colonial Churches are now exercising a mission in regard to the Churches of the West. Thanks to their critique, the churches have discovered to what extent their message, their piety and their institutions have been distorted by colonialist ideology.

The churches in Third World countries strive for a Christian Gospel that expresses solidarity with the poor, the hungry, and the dispossessed, with the masses who have been robbed of their human dignity. They want a Gospel that is not allied with the power of domination. The best known expression of this Christian quest is Latin American liberation theology. Similar liberation theologies exist in all parts of the formerly colonised world. Many elements of this liberation theology have been taken up into the Church's official teaching, especially at the Latin American Bishops Conferences at Medellín (1968) and at Puebla (1979). The so-called 'preferential option for the poor', the decision to look at society from the viewpoint of the victims and to give public witness to solidarity with them, has since been integrated in the Church's official teaching even at the Vatican.[11]

While impressive church documents have been produced, the Christian leaders and theologians who take them with utmost seriousness are still a minority. The Christians in the West who have been most open to liberation theology and the ecclesiastical 'option for the poor', are precisely those who had learnt ideology critique and the need for public witness from their anguished encounter with the Holocaust. In one and the same argument they defend the right to self-determination of the colonised people and the existence of the State of Israel as a place of refuge, a house against death, for a persecuted people. The public policy statements of Christian churches in the United States, including the Catholic Church, affirm the right of Israel to exist in safe borders and all of them, without exception, demand at the same time, human rights for Palestinians and recognise their claim to a homeland.[12] This position is not without its difficulties.

Many Jewish leaders in North America have found this position unacceptable. They have argued that Christians have not sufficiently confronted the Holocaust: they have not yet discerned in themselves their hidden anti-Jewish impulses; they still remain prejudiced in their criticism of Israel; and their defence of Palestinian rights is even-handedness, forgetful of the mortal danger in which the Jewish people find themselves after the murder of the six million. There are undoubtedly Christians who fall into this category. Others do not.

Some Jewish religious leaders have expressed their puzzlement and sometimes even their dismay, at the new political stance taken by the churches in their identification with Latin American liberation movements, with protest movements in the formerly colonised world in general and with the Native peoples and other oppressed groups in North America. In several church documents, the new option has led to a critique of the world capitalist system which protects political freedom and material well being for vast numbers of people at the centre, but which widens the gap between rich countries and poor countries, i.e., creates dependency and misery in the Third World, and even produces ever growing pockets of poverty in the Western industrialised countries.

Emil Fackenheim, the great Jewish religious thinker, who makes response to the Holocaust central in his philosophy and theology, has recently adopted a very critical approach to Christian faith; he has recognised nonetheless the continuity between the Christian response to Auschwitz and the emergence of political and liberation theology.[13] After Auschwitz, he argued, Christians could no longer emphasise the completeness of redemption in Jesus Christ. In the face of the Holocaust, Christians moved into a new sense of unredemption. They recognised the brokenness of the Church, yearned for peace and justice and put their hope in the eschatological promises. Christians began to feel closer to the traditional Jewish longing for the messianic days. Fackenheim's analysis is persuasive. John Pawlikowski has even spoken of a 'contemporary re-Judaisation of Christianity', by which he meant the emergence of an earthly and communal yearning for the fulfilment of the divine promises in history.[14]

The reader will have noticed that this article is written from a North American perspective. It reflects, moreover, my involvement in theological education, located on the whole in the white middle classes. Oppressed groups of people, including oppressed Christians, are likely to look upon the Holocaust quite differently. The Blacks of South Africa who suffer under the brutal system of apartheid and Latin American peasants of Native stock threatened by genocidal action are likely to see in the Holocaust a climactic symbol of the evil empire that now threatens to devour them. Neither the Blacks of South Africa nor the dispossessed Natives of Latin America belong to those who lost their innocence through compromising silence. They were held down as voiceless masses. The Christian preaching they had received was ideologically distorted, including incidentally the anti-Jewish bias; but the main thrust of this ideology was directed against their own group, keeping them tranquil in their house of bondage. The grain of anti-Jewish bias in this preaching must eventually be corrected: but the urgent task of oppressed people is the struggle for their own liberation from Pharoah's domination and the longing for the liberation of all the dominated. How would the Native peoples of Canada react to the Holocaust if they were asked to do so? How do Palestinian Christians react to the Holocaust? How to the Black people of the United States respond to it? How closely do

D

the offspring of African slaves identify with the civilisation that enslaved them? It seems to me more likely that those who are in various ways oppressed look upon the Holocaust as a terrifying event, a fear-creating historical signal, symbolising the extent to which oppressors may go to execute their plans. Samoza had white napalm dropped on his own people in his own city.

The perspective on the Holocaust taken by the oppressed is very close to the position defended by the philosophers of the Frankfurt School. For Adorno and Horkheimer, Auschwitz is not an aberration from Western progress but an exaggeration of present trends operative in Western civilisation, in capitalist societies and in State socialism.[15] Auschwitz gives cruel visibility to the violence built into technological society that produces integration and identity by negating, and if need be, eliminating those who do not fit. For these philosophers Auschwitz contains a judgment on positivistic society. Since Adorno and Horkheimer are not Christians, they have no hesitation in saying this. Christian theologians hesitate to endorse this interpretation because it disguises the part which the Christian tradition has played in the Holocaust.

4. DILEMMA OVER DOUBLE STANDARD

Western Christians of the mainstream are here led to an agonising dilemma. Their encounter with the Holocaust has led them to repentance and great sorrow: they recognise that they must speak out against social evil and examine the complicity of their Church with this social evil. They desire to protect Jews wherever they are endangered. At the same time, the entry into this new self-understanding has compelled them to listen to the voices of all the oppressed. The Christian churches in North America support Israel's right to exist within safe borders and at the same time defend human rights and self-determination for the Palestinians. In this perspective what is needed is an extended ethical debate on policies of compromise.

Many Jewish thinkers in North America have found fault with Christian critics of Israel. They have argued that Christians tend to apply 'a double standard' in their evaluation of Israeli policies. They judge the policies of Israel by a high standard of Jewish and Christian biblical ethics, while they judge the policies of Arab nations and Arab political organisations by purely secular standards defined by the *Realpolitik* of the world. Christians may think that they honour Jews by looking upon the State of Israel as a religious biblical reality: but their use of the double standard in fact damages Israel and may well hide an unacknowledged, hidden, anti-Semitic resentment. Even complete even-handedness is detrimental to Israel, it is argued, because it does not sufficiently recognise the danger in which the State and the Jewish people find themselves in this age.

The accusation certainly applies to many critics of Israel and Israeli policies. But it does not apply to all of them. In particular, the Christians who have reacted to the Holocaust in a manner described in these pages have come to feel uneasy about a totally different ethical 'double standard' that determines their approach to Israel. They have qualms of conscience because they do not apply to Israeli policies the norms by which they judge their own government. When their own government sells arms to Latin American dictators or strengthens its ties with South Africa, these Christians speak out in protest and join pressure groups to persuade the government to change its mind; yet when they read in the press of similar policies adopted by the Israeli government, they tend to remain silent. Christians in the USA and Canada have recently supported the struggle of the Native peoples to gain human rights and have their land claims recognised; yet the same Christians hesitate to be vocal in support of the disinherited Palestinians. Does the discontinuity brought by the Holocaust demand that one live with such an uneasy conscience? Is it a desire for unauthentic continuity to search for ethical principles that strain after universality?

Let it be said that a growing number of Jewish men and women in North America feel equally uneasy about this kind of 'double standard'. They too wish to enter upon an extended ethical debate. While Christians may not feel free to join this discussion, they want to follow it and lean from it.

Rabbi Arthur Hertzberg, an important progressive Jewish spokesman in the United States, has presented an interesting ethical argument to justify this double standard. He recommends that we apply to Israel a policy that in contemporary American legal language is called Affirmative Action.[16] Affirmative Action is a public policy designed to rectify age-old social injustices and discrimination. To correct the exclusion of Blacks or Mexican Americans (or women!) from opportunities to participate and succeed in American institutions, including politics, universities, commerce and industry, Affirmative Action legislation requires that these institutions give preference in hiring to these formerly excluded peoples, even if this inflicts a certain injustice on candidates of the mainstream who are better prepared for the position. To rectify a grave historical evil, Affirmative Action reconciles itself to minor forms of injustice inflicted upon individuals. It is right and just, Rabbi Hertzberg argues, that the West apply Affirmative Action to Israel. But he adds immediately that Affirmative Action has ethical limits. How long should it be applied? And how great are the injustices that may be tolerated?

5. THE MAKING OF PUBLIC POLICY

At present these ethical issues are being debated in Israel. An Israeli organisation, Ox VeShalom, Religious Zionists for Strength and Peace, has introduced this discussion at the heart of Jewish orthodoxy.[17] 'Citizens of Israel, it is up to us to decide what we want', they announce. Then they put the following questions: 'A Jewish State governed by biblical values, just laws and reason OR a garrison state characterised by chauvinism, institutionalised injustice, and xenophobia? A democratic society, flourishing within small borders, in which the Arab minority enjoys full human dignity and human rights OR all of Eretz YIsrael at the price of repressing the political freedoms of one million Palestinian Arabs? Mastery of our collective destiny, in harmony with our neighbours OR dependence on the United States for weapons and money needed to wage war? Mutual recognition and co-existence between Israelis and Palestinians OR escalating destruction and loss of life?'

In North America this ethical debate is just beginning in the Jewish community. Because it has come so late, many Jewish writers demand a return to ethical reflection with great vehemence. In this context I am not thinking of Jewish authors such as Noam Chomsky and T. F. Stone who have always been critical of Zionism and excluded themselves from conversation with the Jewish community. I am thinking, rather, of Jews who are lovers of Israel and as such demand an ethical debate about public policies beyond the double standard. Rabbi Reuben Slonim, a Canadian Zionist, has always criticised Israeli policies and defended Palestinian rights on a Jewish, ethical basis. Thanks to a recent publication he has come into greater prominence in the Jewish community.[18] Earl Shorris, a Jewish novelist, has published a book, *Jews Without Mercy: A Lament*,[19] in which he establishes that Jewish religion has always called for justice and mercy, and then offers a lament that a significant sector of the American Jewish community has turned to the political right, adopted social views contrary to justice and mercy, and allied itself with similar forces in the State of Israel. What he calls for is an ethical debate on public policy. Another Jewish author, Arthur Waskow, also a lover of Israel, is involved in reviving the messianic strain in Jewish religion.[20] He too calls for a critical, ethical debate based on Jewish religious grounds. Some secular authors who define themselves in terms of the Jewish ethical tradition have recently come out with vehement protests. R. S. Feuerlicht's *The Fate of the Jews*[21] accuses the Jewish community of having abandoned ethical thinking in favour of blind loyalty to the Israeli government and therefore of sharing responsibility for the political direction taken by this government, which may ultimately prove to be self-destructive. Many of these critical voices, religious and secular, come together in an organisation of recent origin, the New Jewish Agenda.

The debate on ethical imperatives has taken place in Jewish religious literature in terms of the appropriate response to the Holocaust experience. For Jewish religious thinkers the Holocaust has a never to be relativised singularity, a uniqueness that will mark Jewish self-understanding forever. They resist the social scientific tendency to compare the Holocaust with other mass crimes in history—other genocides, mass bombings, and planned famines—as if the Holocaust were just one horror among a list of horrors. The Jewish thinkers resist this as an attempt to disguise the full demonic power revealed in the Holocaust and make less grave Western responsibility for the event. For Jewish religious authors the summons coming from the Holocaust says, 'Never again!' For some this means, Never again shall the Jewish people be humiliated and destroyed, and for others it means, never again shall the Jewish people nor any powerless people be humiliated and destroyed. The difference between the two is considerable.[22] The latter group of thinkers argue that the unparalleled, never-to-be relativised singularity of the Holocaust gives rise to a Jewish response that has universal implications and provides ethical guidelines for public policies. The Jewish religious authors for whom the summons, 'Never again!' refers exclusively to the future of the Jewish people tend to remain silent on the urgent contemporary issues such as the nuclear arms race, world hunger, the genocides of Native peoples in Latin America, apartheid in South Africa, and so forth.

The philosopher Emil Fackenheim has not resolved his own ambivalence on this topic. He insists that there shall be no relativising of the Holocaust and argues that Jews must resist a universalist ethical approach that would weaken them in their stubborn, faithful struggle for survival. He feels no urgency to take sides in the ethical debates on such issues as nuclear war, world hunger, or military dictatorships. He tends to evaluate historical events, in obedience to the summons from the Holocaust, in terms of the effect they have on the security of Israel and the Jewish people. At the same time, he speaks repeatedly of the present as the 'age of Auschwitz and Hiroshima'. In a moving passage he declares that Jews cannot say 'May the horror that has come upon us never come upon you,' to accomplices of the Holocaust nor to the silent by-standers, but they 'can and must say [this] to those upon whom it, or something resembling it, has come—starving African children, Gulag slave labourers, boat people roaming the seas.'[23] Here Fackenheim does not think that speaking of 'it, or something resembling it', implies a relativisation of the Holocaust. On the contrary, it is for him a starting point for more universal ethical reflection.

In recent years Jewish authors have been greatly concerned about the abuse of Holocaust language. They fear that contemporary political issues are often resolved not by a rational debate on ethics and strategy but by remembering the Holocaust and reacting to the present as if it were the past. Such abuse has become very widespread. The Western press has often described the Israeli occupation of the West Bank and the more recent Israeli invasion of Lebanon in terms drawn from Nazi aggression during the Second World War, implying that Jews have become like the Nazis who persecuted them. Jewish and some Christian voices have protested against this. The same unfortunate trend, however, is also found in the State of Israel. Mr Menachem Begin set the tone for this. In his public utterance during the summer of 1982, Beirut became 'Berlin', and his military campaign set out to destroy 'Hitler' in his 'bunker deep beneath the surface'.[24]

During the war in Lebanon, even the debate in Israel itself deteriorated to name-calling that drew upon Nazi memories. In the pro-Begin Likud attacks on the Peace Now Movement, the murdered peace demonstrator Emil Grunzweig was compared to Horst Wessel, a member of the Hitler Youth murdered by communists who was made into a martyr of the Nazi movement. The opponents of the Begin government also occasionally used analogies drawn from the Nazis. Thus some opposed the Jewish settlements on the West Bank as creating a *Herrenvolk* democracy.[25] In Jerusalem and Tel Aviv swastikas are occasionally painted on house walls by Sephardic militants or ultra-Orthodox groups as a protest against the Israeli police.[26]

In response to these abuses Abba Eban has insisted that since the Holocaust is an altogether unique event, it is not licit to use analogies drawn from this event in debates dealing with contemporary policies. 'Under Mr Begin Israeli relations with other countries have ceased to be regarded as similar to other international relations, whether concerned with co-operation, opposition or even confrontation. With Mr Begin and his cohorts, every foe becomes a 'Nazi', and every blow becomes an 'Auschwitz'.[27] Other Jewish voices have complained that Holocaust language is used to justify contemporary political policies. Nathan Goldmann, one time president of the World Jewish Congress and the World Zionist Organization, said that 'the use of the Holocaust as an argument to justify politically doubtful and morally indefensible policies is a kind of *hillul hasham*, a banalisation of the Holocaust.[28] Abba Eban has asked for the end of Holocaust language in the political arena.

Today some religious thinkers in Israel have questioned whether the Holocaust should be at the centre of Jewish theology at all. While the mass murder of the six million must never be forgotten and fade from Jewish consciousness, the Holocaust cannot be the foundation for a religious revival of Judaism.[29] A similar point of view has been defended by some Jewish religious thinkers in the United States and in Britain.[30] The Holocaust does not summon forth the kind of inspiration and ethical commitment a people need to define their collective identity and their historical future. Jewish religious renewal must be grounded in the Mount Sinai experience, God's covenant with the people of Israel. Jews who assign a central place to the Holocaust argue that this uniquely evil event has introduced discontinuity in human history, and that it is illusory and even dangerous for Jews to aspire to an ethical religion of universal meaning as if nothing had happened.

What does the discontinuity produced by the Holocaust mean to Jews and to Christians? Are there some continuities that must be defended against inappropriate shattering? Christians at this time are involved in a theological debate over the relation between biblical faith and public policy. It seems to me that Jewish religious thinkers are moving to a similar debate among themselves. Can it be said that Jews and Christians have become brothers (sisters) in a new way because in their own communities they wrestle with similar issues?

Notes

1. Rosemary Ruether *Faith and Fratricide*, (New York 1974).

2. *Origins, NC Documentary Service*, vol. 13, no. 1, p. 27. In the debate Bishop Hunthausen said that the Trident located in his diocese can destroy as many as 408 separate areas, each with a bomb five times more powerful than the one dropped on Hiroshima. The Trident and the MX missile have such accuracy and power, he said, that they can only be understood as first-strike nuclear weapons. 'I say with deep consciousness of these words that Trident is the Auschwitz of Puget Sound.' (Jim Castelli *The Bishops and the Bomb*, Garden City, NY 1983, p. 28.)

3. J. B. Metz 'Oekumene nach Auschwitz' in *Gott nach Auschwitz* ed. Eugen Kogon (Freiburg 1983). pp. 121–144.

4. J. Moltmann *The Experiment Hope* (Philadelphia 1975).

5. D. Soelle 'Theology and Liberation' in *Political Theology in the Canadian Context*, ed. B. Smillie (Waterloo, Ont. 1982), p. 113.

6. R. McAfee Brown 'The Holocaust as a Problem in Moral Choices' in *When God and Man Failed* ed. H. Cargas (Philadelphia 1981), pp. 81–102.

7. F. Fiorenza *Foundational Theology* (New York 1984).

8. M. Lamb *Solidarity With Victims* (New York 1982).

9. Rosemary Ruether *Liberation Theology* (New York 1972), pp. 65–94.

10. M. Horkheimer & T. Adorno *Dialectic of Enlightenment* (New York 1972), pp. 168–208.

11. See G. Baum 'Faith and Liberation: Development Since Vatican II' in *Vatican II: Open Questions and New Horizons* ed. G. Fagin (Wilmington, DE 1984), pp. 75–104.

12. A. Solomonov *Where We Stand: Official Statements of American Churches on the Middle East Conflict* (The Middle East Consulting Group, 339 Lafayette St., New York, N.Y. 1977). See also 'The Middle East: The Pursuit of Peace with Justice', National Conference of Catholic Bishops, Washington, DC 1978.

13. Emil Fackenheim *To Mend the World* (New York 1982), pp. 285–286.

14. John Pawlikowski *Sinai and Calvary* (Beverley Hills, Ca. 1976), p. 222.

15. See M. Lamb *Solidarity With Victims* (New York 1982), pp. 38–39.

16. Proceedings of the 5th National Workshop on Jewish-Christian Relations, Texas, 1980 (tapes).

17. *Oz VeShalom* (P.O. Box 4433, Jerusalem, Israel 91043), English-language bulletin no. 2, November 1982.

18. R. Slonim *Grand to be an orphan* (Toronto 1983).

19. E. Shorris *Jews Without Mercy: A Lament* (Garden City, NY 1982).

20. A. Waskow *These Holy Sparks: The Rebirth of the Jewish People* (San Francisco 1983).

21. R. S. Feuerlicht *The Fate of the Jews: A People Torn Between Israeli Power and Jewish Ethics* (New York 1983).

22. G. Baum *The Social Imperative* (New York 1979), pp. 39–69.

23. E. Fackenheim, the work cited in note 13, p. 306.

24. M. R. Marrus 'Is There a New Antisemitism?' *Middle East Focus* 6, no 4 (November 1983), 14.

25. *Ibid.*

26. *Ibid.*

27. *Ibid.*, pp. 15–16.

28. R. Slonim, the work cited in note 18, p. 152.

29. David Hartman 'Auschwitz or Sinai? *The Jerusalem Post*, Oct. 12, 1982. See *The Ecumenist* 21, no. 1, pp 6–8.

30. Jacob Neusner *Stranger at Home: The Holocaust, Zionism and American Judaism* (Chicago 1981). Dow Marmur *Beyond Survival; Reflections on the Future of Judaism* (London 1982).

John Pawlikowski

The Holocaust and Contemporary Christology

1. ORIENTATIONS: AUSCHWITZ IN CONTEMPORARY JEWISH AND CHRISTIAN THINKING

ANYONE EVEN minimally acquainted with directions in contemporary Jewish thought will recognise that the Nazi Holocaust has come to play a central role in reflections on present-day Jewish religious identity. There certainly exist significant differences of interpretation among the principal commentators who include Irving Greenberg, Emil Fackenheim, Richard Rubenstein, Arthur Cohen and Elie Wiesel, to name but a few.

Most Orthodox Jewish writers such as Michael Wyschograd have not thought it possible to advance the theological discussion of the Holocaust beyond the traditional category of evil, admitting, however, that the monstrous nature of Auschwitz comes close to breaking the classical parameters of this category. Non-Orthodox theologians and some at the far edges of contemporary Jewish Orthodoxy such as Irving Greenberg have called for some measure of faith reformulation after the Holocaust. Recently some challenges to the theological centrality of the Holocaust have begun to emerge in non-Orthodox circles, principally in the writings of Eugene Borowitz. In his recent volume *Choices in Modern Jewish Thought: A Partisan Guide*[1] Borowitz argues that the Holocaust must be re-integrated into a more primary discussion—the continued meaning of the commanding presence of the convenantal God and its relationship to personal autonomy in faith expression. It is the latter, personal autonomy, that he defines as the central reality of Jewish theological reflection today.

The ferment about the religious significance of the Holocaust will no doubt continue for some time to come. It is a debate that Christian theologians will need to follow closely. I continue to stand by the thesis that the Holocaust is what Irving Greenberg has called an 'orienting event' for contemporary theology. The challenge to this claim by Borowitz and others, while raising some critical questions which need attention, fails to deal adequately with theology's relationship to history and to grasp the profound connection between 'personal autonomy' and Auschwitz.

Turning now to the Holocaust's significance for Christian theological reflection one reality seems clear. Given the centrality of Christology in Christian faith expression the Holocaust must have implications for this dimension of Christian faith or it can hardly be termed an 'orienting event'.

Thus far few systematic theologians have seen it as such. Eva Fleischner rightly criticises

43

this silence about the Holocaust in post-Auschwitz systematic theology, especially in Germany, in her volume *Judaism in German Christian Theology since 1945*.[2] A few have spoken with admirable sensitivity about the sufferings of Jews at the hands of the Nazis. Hans Küng is one example. But this concern has had little if any direct impact on basic theological formulation. The Holocaust never receives a mention in the Christological discussions of liberationist theologians despite some heightened sense in Gutierrez and Bonino about the positive links between the Exodus covenantal tradition of the Hebrew Scriptures and the freedom central to the Christ Event.

Recently a few Christian theologians have begun to wrestle with the theological dimensions of Auschwitz. And the implications for Christology have emerged as a major focus for most. This group includes Franklin Sherman, Marcel Dubois, Gregory Baum, David Tracy, Douglas J. Hall, Clemens Thoma and in a particular way Jürgen Moltmann whose *The Crucified God*[3] represents the first comprehensive attempt at Christological statement that takes the Holocaust experience with utmost seriousness. Much of the initial attempt to relate the Holocaust to Christology has centred on its connection with the suffering motif of the Cross. I will return to this connection later on in this essay.

Within the context of these contemporary developments in Holocaust theology in both Judaism and Christianity I would now like to lay out one possible model for theological linkage between Auschwitz and the Christ Event. To do this, it will be necessary to sketch briefly my general approach to the implications for theology inherent in the Holocaust.

2. THE FOUNDATIONS OF A DEVELOPED APPROACH

I have been persuaded by scholars such as the Israeli historian Uriel Tal that the Holocaust represents something more than the final, albeit most gruesome, sequel in the long, tragic narrative of Christian anti-Semitism. There is no question that Christian anti-Semitism provided an indispensable seedbed for Nazism in making Jews the primary and special victims of its onslaught on humanity. But also involved in the Holocaust was the plan to create a 'new person', a super being, in a social setting which found growing technological competency combining with bureaucratic efficiency and the erosion of traditional religious restraints upon human behaviour to open the doors to virtually unlimited and morally unchallenged use of power to reshape human society and even the human person. Though the Nazis used Christian churches and Christian leaders in some instances in their primal attack on the Jews, their philosophy at its depth was decidedly anti-Christian as well as anti-Jewish. And their calculated genocidal plan for 'renewing' humankind listed Gay people, Gypsies and the mentally/physically handicapped for extermination, as well as the subjugation of the Slavs, especially the Polish nation.

The challenge to human integrity as well as to any notion of a loving, caring God assumes even greater proportions when we recognise that it was some of the best educated people in a society many considered among the most advanced yet generated by the human spirit who fashioned this 'social development'. Auschwitz was not simply the creation of raving idiots or classical political despots. Leo Kuper speaks well to this especially sinister component of the Holocaust in his volume *Genocide: its Political use in the Twentieth Century*:

> Then there was the extreme bureaucratic organisation of the genocide. This was one of its most dehumanised aspects. . . . But to use bureaucratic planning and procedures and regulation for a massive operation of systematic murder throughout a whole continent speaks of an almost inconceivably profound dehumanisation.[4]

Auschwitz truly opened up a new era in human possibility. The perpetrators of the

Holocaust seized upon the destructive side of this possibility. In so doing they challenged many traditional Christian theological notions that had previously grounded the conduct of human affairs. They passed beyond many previous barriers in their use of human power and ingenuity. They clearly showed that religious concepts, including fundamental God-concepts, which had dominated human consciousness since biblical times were waning in their influence.

The fundamental reality that has emerged from my research into the Holocaust is the *new sense of human freedom present among the Nazi theoreticians.* The Nazis had correctly assessed modern human experience in at least one crucial respect. They rightly understood that profound changes were at work in human consciousness. Under the impact of the new science and technology, the human community was starting to undergo a transformation that can aptly be described as Prometheus Unbound, and that on a mass scale.

An awareness was beginning to build of a degree of human autonomy and power far greater than most of Christian theology had allowed for in the past. It is precisely for this reason that Borowitz's setting up of personal autonomy as a competing problem for centrality in contemporary theological reflection with the holocaust misses a vital connection. As I see it, human autonomy is the principal theological issue to arise out of reflection on the Auschwitz experience.

In the Nazi perception the possibility now existed to reshape human society, perhaps humanity itself, to an extent never previously imaginable. This new possibility created a new responsibility—to liberate humankind from the 'polluters' of authentic humanity, the dregs of society, as these were arbitrarily determined by the Master Race. People now began to use death to solve the problem of human existence. As Uriel Tal has maintained, the 'Final Solution' was meant to answer an universal crisis of the human person. It aimed at a total transformation of human values at the heart of which was the loosing of the 'shackles' of the historic God-idea with its attendant notions of moral responsibility, redemption, sin and revelation.

In the light of the Holocaust and related examples of the brutalisation of human power it is incumbent upon contemporary Christianity to devise ways to affirm the new sense of freedom that is continuing to dawn within mankind while channelling it into constructive outlets. Post-Holocaust Christian faith expression must fully recognise and welcome this development of a new sense of human liberation and elevation as a positive and central part of the process of human salvation. But the Nazi experience will of necessity mute any wild applause for this new sense of human freedom. The challenge facing Christianity is whether it can now provide an understanding and experience of the God-human person relationship which can guide this newly discovered power and freedom constructively and creatively. Somehow faith encounter and faith expression today must be such that they can prevent the newly discovered creative power of humanity from being transformed into the destructive force we have seen exposed in all its ugliness in the Holocaust.

For this to happen in a meaningful way we shall have to recover *a fresh sense of transcendence.* Men and women will once more need to experience contact with a personal power beyond themselves, a power that heals the destructive tendencies still lurking within humanity. The Holocaust has destroyed simplistic 'commanding God' notions. Here is a point where I find myself much closer to Irving Greenberg and Arthur Cohen than to Eugene Borowitz who continues the 'commanding God' language. But the Holocaust will not leave us satisfied with their positions as now stated nor with the more radical position of Richard Rubenstein. It has exposed our desperate need to retain a sense of a 'compelling God', *compelling* because we have experienced through symbolic encounter with this God a healing, a strengthening, an affirming that buries any need to assert our humanity through the destructive, even deathly, use of human power. It is a God to whom we are drawn, rather than a God who imposes on us. This sense of a compelling Parent God who has gifted humanity, who shares in our vulnerability through the Cross, is the foundation for any adequate moral ethos in contemporary society. Thus I feel that there is no meaningful discussion of the Holocaust's impact on Christology without first raising the Auschwitz-God connection. David Tracy is perfectly correct in the following observation:

> . . . As far as I am aware, the ultimate theological issue, the understanding of God, has yet to receive much reflection from Catholic theologians. And yet, as Schleirmacher correctly insisted, the doctrine of God can never be 'another' doctrine for theology, but must pervade all doctrines. Here Jewish theology in its reflections on the reality of God since the *tremendum* of the Holocaust, has led the way for all serious theological reflection.[5]

Any relevant discussion of Christology needs to relate the Christ Event directly to the God-problem resulting from the Holocaust experience. Such relationships, in so far as they have been constructed thus far, centre, as we have already seen, on the Cross and its links with the sufferings of the Jewish people: Lutheran ethicist Franklin Sherman has uncovered in the Cross of Christ 'the symbol of the agonising God'. The only legitimate theodicy for Sherman in the light of the Holocaust is one that grasps in the Christ Event the revelation of divine participation in the sufferings of people who are in turn summoned to take part in the sufferings of God. 'We speak of God after Auschwitz', Sherman insists, 'only as the one who calls us to a new unity as between brothers—not only between Jews and Christians, but especially between Jews and Christians'.[6]

Douglas Hall strikes a similar note. After the Holocaust the theology of the Cross alone expresses the thorough meaning of the Incarnation. Only this Christological emphasis truly establishes the authentic divine-human link implied in the Word becoming flesh by emphasising the solidarity of God with suffering humanity. Integrated with the Holocaust experience of Christology with the Cross as its central focus establishes a soteriology of solidarity which sets up the Cross of Jesus as a point of fraternal union with the Jewish people, and with all who seek human liberation and peace, not as a point of exclusion:

> . . . The faith of Israel is incomprehensible unless one sees at its heart a suffering God whose solidarity with humanity is so abysmal that the 'cross in the heart of God' (H. Wheeler Robinson) must always be incarnating itself in history. Reading the works of Elie Wiesel, one knows, as a Christian, that he bears this indelible resemblance to the people of Israel.[7]

The most comprehensive treatment of the Christology-Holocaust link thus far has come in the writings of Jurgen Moltmann, especially *The Crucified God*. He interprets Auschwitz as the most dramatic revelation to date of the fundamental meaning of the Christ Event—God can save people, including Israel, because through the Cross he participated in their very suffering. To theologise after the Holocaust would prove a futile enterprise in Moltmann's view

> . . . were not the *Sch'ma Israel* and the Lord's Prayer prayed in Auschwitz itself, were not God himself in Auschwitz, suffering with the martyred and murdered. Every other answer would be blasphemy. An absolute God would make us indifferent. The God of action and success would let us forget the dead, which we still cannot forget. God as nothingness would make the entire world into a concentration camp.[8]

Moltmann adds that the 'theology of divine vulnerability' that emerges from a reflection on the Shoah, the preferred term for the Holocaust in some Jewish circles, has deep roots in both rabbinic theology and in Abraham Heschel's notion of *divine pathos*.

The theology of divine vulnerability provides an important starting point for a post-Holocaust Christology. For one, it establishes the close link between Christology and the more fundamental God-problem. It likewise opens up the whole question of dual responsibility—divine and human—during the Holocaust. Too often, as Holocaust interpreter Elie Wiesel himself has noted, the onus has been placed only on God's shoulders. The Holocaust, let is be said clearly, is also a challenge to any naively positive interpretation of human capacity. The Cross emphasis in Holocaust theology exposes us to the notion that God had to pay a price for the freedom accorded when humankind abused this freedom as it did in massive fashion in the Holocaust.

But there are aspects to a Holocaust theology focused on the Cross that leave the sensitive Christian uneasy. There has to be some question about the propriety of combining the theology of the Cross with the Auschwitz experience in view of the significant Christian complicity in the Nazi effort. A. Roy Eckardt is especially strong on this point, arguing that it approaches blasphemy to make such a claim. He also believes that 'in comparison with certain other sufferings, Jesus' death becomes relatively non-significant'. Another danger Eckardt sees in the Christology as Cross model after the Holocaust is that it may generate an exaggeratedly 'powerless' plan for human living within a religious context that could result in the annihilation of both Jews and Christians.[9] Additionally, Christian theology has always described the Cross as a voluntary act on the part of God and Jesus; the Cross can be interpreted in a redemptive fashion when seen as the culmination and the consequence of Jesus' active ministry. Auschwitz was neither voluntary nor redemptive in any sense. Finally, some doubts have also been raised whether the theology of divine suffering found in Jewish religious thought is as similar to the Holocaust Cross theology as Moltmann and Sherman claim.

Eckardt has overdrawn his criticism of the theology of the Cross after the Holocaust, though many of his objections must be taken seriously. The answer is to integrate the perspectives offered by Moltmann, Sherman, Hall and others into a broader Christological vision. It is a vision that I have tried to delineate in a preliminary fashion in my volume *Christ in the Light of the Christian-Jewish Dialogue*.[10] It revolves around an understanding that the reality of the Incarnation, the Word made flesh, is far more central to the Christ Event than any Messianic fulfilment claims.

3. ONE POSSIBLE MODEL FOR LINKING AUSCHWITZ TO THE CHRIST EVENT

Understanding the ministry of Jesus as emerging from the heightened sense of divine-human intimacy that surfaced in the Pharisaic revolution in Second Temple Judaism, the Christological claims made by the Church in reflection on that ministry tried to express a new sense of how profoundly humanity is imbedded in the divine self-definition. The ultimate significance of this Christology lies in its revelation of the grandeur of humanity, a necessary corrective to the demeaning paternalism that often characterised the divine–human relationship in the past.

In my view the fear and paternalism associated in the past with the statement of the divine–human relationship were at least partially responsible for the attempt by Nazism to produce a total reversal of human meaning, to go back to Uriel Tal's analysis, and finally overpower the Creator God. Incarnational Christology can help the human person realise that he or she shares in the very life and existence of God. The human person remains creature; the gulf between humanity in people and humanity in the Godhead has not been bridged. But it is also clear that a direct link exists; the two humanities can touch. The human struggles for self-identity vis-a-vis the Creator God has come to an end in principle, though its full realisation still lies ahead. In this sense one can truly say that Christ continues to bring humankind salvation in its root meaning—*wholeness*.

With a proper understanding of the meaning of the Christ Event men and women can be healed, they can finally overcome the primal sin of pride, the desire to supplant the Creator in power and status that was at the heart of the Holocaust. Critical to this awareness is the sense of God's self-imposed limitation as manifested in the Cross. This is where Moltmann's theology becomes absolutely crucial, if still incomplete. People now see, through Christ, that their destiny is eternal in their uniqueness and individuality. God will not finally try to absorb them totally back into the divine being. In fact, it has become apparent that God must allow men and women this degree of eternal distinctiveness and freedom of action in order to reach full maturity, to become finally and fully God. This is a viewpoint, incidentally, that finds echoes in the Jewish mystical literature which speaks of God's self-constriction in the choice to become Creator.

What I am claiming is that the Holocaust represents at one and the same time the ultimate expression of human freedom and of evil—the two are intimately linked. The initial divine act of creation constituted the liberation of humanity from its total encasement in the Godhead. The Creator God acknowledged that there is need to let go part of divine humanity as part of the development of the divine creative potential. But that part of God's humanity that now assumed an independent existence was faced with the task of establishing its own identity. At times there was a strong desire to supplant the Creator. Here lie the roots of human evil. But until the modern age fear of divine punishment kept such a desire in check. But the Enlightenment, Nietzsche and other contemporary movements of human liberation changed all that. People began to lose the fear of divine retribution that had controlled human behaviour in the past. The Nazis clearly believed they had become the final arbiters of right and wrong. This new sense of freedom, this growing Prometheus-Unbound experience, in Western society, coupled with unresolved identity problems within humanity resulted in a catastrophic plan of human destruction in Nazi Germany. The ultimate assertion of human freedom from God in our time that the Holocaust represents may in fact prove the beginning of the final resolution of the conflict. When humanity finally recognises the destruction it can produce when it totally rejects its Creator, as it did in the Holocaust, when it recognises such rejection as a perversion not an affirmation of human freedom, a new stage in human consciousness may be dawning. We may finally be coming to grips with evil at its roots, the centuries-long struggle of the human community to work out its identity by overcoming God. The power of evil will wane only when humankind develops along with a sense of profound dignity because of its links with God through Christ, a corresponding sense of humility occasioned by a searching encounter with the devastation it is capable of producing when left to its own wits. A sense of profound humility evoked by the experience of the healing power present in the ultimate Creator of human power—this is crucial. On this point of humility as a critical response to the Holocaust experience I join hands with the ethicist Stanley Hauerwas in his reflections on Auschwitz even though we part company on several implications of the event.[11]

Only the integration of this awareness of humility into human consciousness will finally overcome evil and neutralise attempts such as the Holocaust in which humanity tries to 'elevate' itself above the Creator. This human self-realisation will come easier in light of the understanding of divine vulnerability that the Holocaust made manifest in such a dramatic fashion. It is no longer 'ungodly' to express dependence upon others—the Creator has done it. The full maturity vital for the humane exercise of human co-creatorship requires the assertion of this interdependence to which the Nazis were blind.

Let me add that the ultimate personal healing resulting from a proper understanding of Incarnational Christology must also be tied, for full wholeness and salvation, to the sense of communal interdependence revealed by the Sinai covenant. Though this chapter has centred on Christology and the Holocaust, any post-Holocaust significance for Christology must be stated in the context of Christianity's continuing links to Judaism and other world religions. At this point in time it must be admitted that the believing Jew and the believing Christian may cast post-Holocaust theology in somewhat different directions. This is an issue that cannot be elaborated here. But it needs to be emphasised that the above preliminary reflections on the significance of Christology in no way mean to imply that there is no theological response for believers to the experience of the Holocaust except through Christology. This appears to be a trap into which Moltmann has wandered in *The Crucified God*.

The Holocaust has unquestionably undercut many conventional Christological claims. It has rendered any Christological approach that portrays Jews and Judaism as religious relics a moral obscenity. It also forces us to appreciate more intensely God's dependence on the human community—something implied in the 'Abba' experience of God which Edward Schillebeeckx has developed so thoroughly. And 'optimistic' theologians such as the liberationists need to treat much more seriously demonic events like Auschwitz.

But the core meaning of Christology remains despite the Holocaust. In fact I would contend that this core meaning has become even more urgent in the light of Auschwitz, which increasingly we are coming to appreciate not merely as an isolated period in modern history but as a turning point, a new era, in which the combination of technological advancement, bureaucratic growth and the weakening of traditional moral restraints has coalesced to render massive human destruction an ever-present possibility.

Notes

1. New York 1983.
2. Metuchen, NJ 1975.
3. New York 1974.
4. New Haven, Conn. 1984, p. 120.
5. 'Religious Values after the Holocaust: A Catholic View,' in Abraham, *Jews and Christians after the Holocaust* ed J. Peck (Philadelphia 1982) p. 101.
6. 'Speaking of God after Auschwitz' *Worldview* 17, 9 (September 1974), 29. Also see Sherman's essay on the same theme in *Speaking of God Today* ed. Paul D. Opsahl and Marc H. Tanenbaum (Philadelphia 1974).
7. 'Rethinking Christ' in *Antisemitism and the Foundations of Christianity* ed. Alan T. Davies (New York 1979), p. 183.
8. 'The Crucified God' *Theology Today* 31, 1 (April 1974) 9.
9. 'Christians and Jews: Along a Theological Frontier' *Encounter* 40, 2 (Spring 1979) 102.
10. Ramsey, NJ 1982.
11. 'Jews and Christians Among the Nations' *Cross Currents* 31 (Spring 1981) 34.

PART III

Biblical Studies

Luise Schottroff

Anti-Judaism in the New Testament

THE WAY the New Testament has been used throughout the history of the Church in Germany, Western Europe and the Western world as a whole has involved it in the culpable anti-Judaism which has been a feature of the Church and of theology. In Germany, even after Auschwitz, the extent of this heinous influence has not been recognised. Apart from a few admonitory voices, theological anti-Judaism remained intact in NT scholarship because there was no awareness of the problem. It was felt that theological anti-Judaism was not the same thing as anti-Semitism. 'It is quite possible to admire and appreciate the Jews and to affirm and actively promote the State of Israel without needing to find a '*heilsgeschichtlich*' basis for such an approach, and without sacrificing or even relativising the fundamental Christian truths which separate Christianity and Judaism'—so we read in a response by members of the Faculty of Evangelical Theology of the University of Bonn to the 1980 'Synodal Statement on Renewal of the Relationship between Christians and Jews' of the Rhineland (Evangelical) Church.

People are only now beginning to realise that, right up to the present day, the Christian interpretation of the NT has been making use of negative clichés about the Jewish religion in formulating these 'fundamental Christian truths'. Such awareness is growing in the churches rather than in the theological faculties. The few clear statements issued from within German Evangelical biblical studies still represent a minority view (e.g. P. von der Osten-Sacken, 'Von der Notwendigkeit theologischen Besitzverzichtes', a postscript to the German edition of R. Ruether's *Faith and Fratricide* (New York 1974): *Nächstenliebe und Brudermord. Die theologischen Wurzeln des Antisemitismus* (Munich 1978), pp. 244–251). The idea that a 'renunciation of possessions' (*Besitzverzicht*) is involved rightly shows that attempting to overcome theological anti-Judaism—in NT hermeneutics too—actually disturbs the roots of Christian self-understanding. In this context we have only just begun to come to grips, historically and theologically, with the anti-Judaism of the NT. The following are some initial reflections on three NT topics.

1. JESUS AND THE PHARISEES

In dealing with the NT we must clearly distinguish two questions: (a) What form of anti-Judaism does the NT itself exhibit? (b) How can we overcome the anti-Judaism which has characterised the history of Christian NT hermeneutics? There is no such thing as a positivistic hermeneutics—question (a) cannot be answered objectively, non-judgmentally, purely from a historian's point of view—so both questions are interrelated. For the sake of clarity, however, they are best considered separately.

The pejorative term 'Pharisee' is a constant feature of NT interpretation. Here I cite a crucial text in order to ask historically and theologically about the relationship of Jesus to the Pharisees without making the prior assumption that 'the Pharisees' were representatives of a works-oriented religious legalism. What is the implication of Mark 2:27: 'And he said to them [i.e. the Pharisees], "The sabbath was made for man, not man for the sabbath" '? Hermeneutical tradition consistently sees this pronouncement as a fundamental critique of the Pharisees' sabbath teaching and practice. Here Jesus 'clearly puts all sabbath regulations in question' and expresses 'profound opposition to Pharisaic thought' (H. Merkel 'Jesus und die Pharisäer' in *NTS* 14, 1967/8, p. 204). The conflict found in the text is understood as a deep doctrinal conflict (and the view quoted is also representative of the modern approach in hermeneutics): the Pharisees have a false attitude to God and 'man' and, arising from it, their legal code is an inhuman one (see e.g. R. Pesch *Das Markusevangelium* 1 (Freiburg 1976) p. 196: 'Both Jesus and Paul condemn the inhuman casuistry of a perverted religious obedience'). Now there is a strikingly similar rabbinic parallel to Mark 2:27: 'The sabbath was given to you, not you to the sabbath (*Mechiltha* on Exod. 31:14), i.e., the saving of human life 'suppresses' the sabbath, takes precedence over the command to keep the sabbath holy. The Christian interpretation of Mark 2:27 sees this rabbinic dictum as the justification for casuistic exceptions. Jesus' dictum, on the other hand, is held to be a fundamental questioning of all sabbath regulations 'in so far as they do not minister to human beings' (R. Pesch *ibid.*, p. 184). The influential Strack/Billerbecki *Kommentar zum Neuen Testament aus Talmud und Midrasch* (I, p. 622 ff.) expressed this style of hermeneutics and gave an anti-Judaistic slant to whole generations of textual interpretation. (This is not to minimise the scholarly value of this commentary, which is 'only' echoing the anti-Judaism of NT scholarship in general.) The rabbinic teaching is thus understood as a solution for a particular concrete situation, whereas Jesus' pronouncement is seen as the first prong of a fundamentally new doctrine. Clearly this is to isolate the content of Mark 2:27 from its literary context. This is the only way in which such a conclusion could be drawn.

In my view such a state of affairs calls for a fundamental methodological critique and a change in procedures. There is an absolute necessity to observe the text's *literary context* and *life context*. The literary context in the narrower sense (Mark 2:23–28) describes a conflict between Jesus and the Pharisees on account of the disciples', who had been plucking ears of corn on the sabbath, blowing the chaff away and eating the raw cornseed. They were hungry and did not keep to the commandment prohibiting them from preparing food on the sabbath. Mark 2:27 is not the initial attack of a whole campaign at the level of principle but a second biblical argument following the one in Mark 2:25 f., which Jesus cites in theological justification of his disciples' action. Far from making a radical attack on the Pharisees, the argument we have in the text invites them to agree on theological grounds. Jesus is arguing on the same theological basis as his interlocutors: the authority of scripture, the Torah. He quotes I Sam. 21:1–7 (in Mark 2:25 f.) and the Genesis creation account (in Mark 2:27). Danger to life suppresses sabbath regulations: this is not disputed between him and the Pharisees. What *is* in dispute is the concrete situation: Are the disciples in such straits that they may break the sabbath? It is impossible to understand the text at this point without ascertaining the life-context. In a world in which famine is an everyday occurrence, and where an entire population lives in poverty, the disciples' hunger is quite different from what it has become in Christian interpretation, i.e., a random instance chosen to provoke a fundamental doctrinal conflict. Jesus endeavours to persuade the Pharisees to acknowledge, theologically, that such hunger takes precedence over the sabbath because it is against God's will for people to suffer hunger. Mark 2:23–27 describes a symbolic infringement of regulations by Jesus and his disciples which actually presupposes a basic agreement in the teaching of both sides. The Jesus of this story is the Saviour of the Poor and not the Preacher of a new teaching about God and 'man'.

Jesus' closeness to the Pharisees in this story contrasts remarkably with the role of the Pharisees in the literary macro-context, the Gospel of Mark. According to Mark's Gospel it was because of these and other, similar conflicts that 'the Pharisees . . . and the Herodians' determined that Jesus should die (Mark 3:6). Much of this view is historically inaccurate; above all, as the synoptic Passion narratives show, the Pharisees were not actively involved in the sentencing and execution of Jesus.

As this example makes clear, the problem of theological anti-Judaism in the synoptic gospels arises at the level of the macro-context. Mark 3:6 and the Gospel of Mark, Matt. 23 and the Gospel of Matthew sound a harsh and discordant note particularly in the dispute with the Pharisees. In coming to grips with this plain fact we need to bear the following in mind: (a) The synoptic gospels are the product of a history, the history of the Jesus movement. Within this, the dispute with the Pharisees also underwent a recognisable development. At the time of Jesus the Pharisees played a different role, even among their own people, from that after the destruction of the Temple and the Jewish-Roman war of 66–70 A.D. At the level of the macro-context the mutual antagonism is much fiercer than in Jesus' own time. Jews felt that the Jewish Christians and Gentile Christians threatened their own religious identity. Above all the coexistence of Jewish Christians and the uncircumcised in the community gave rise to persecution (see Gal. 2:11–14), Christians accuse Jews of being responsible for the death of Jesus (see Mark 3:6) and of having rejected God's Messiah, as we find stressed on every page of Matthew's Gospel. There are different views as to when a 'Christian' awareness, as opposed to a 'Jewish' awareness, came about. The Gospel of Matthew's harsh criticism of the Pharisees uses the prophetic idiom, announcing judgment against the obstinate and faithless people of God. For 'Matthew', therefore, it will be necessary to speak of a conflict between Christians and Jews rather than of an internal Jewish conflict. For 'Mark', although earlier in date, the distance is probably greater than for 'Matthew'.

What is the hermeneutical significance of this brief outline? At all events, it is one thing to speak about 'the Jews' against the background of Christianity's long history as a Church and a powerful factor in the world, and quite another to be Jewish or Gentile Christians at the end of the first century, in fundamental conflict with Jews. For there was a concrete issue in this latter conflict, namely, the significance of the Messiah, Jesus, for the everyday life and social interaction of his Gentile and Jewish followers. It is in this sense that Jesus' Messiahship became the disputed point. On the other side the Jews were bound to see Christianity as a threat, abetting the integration of Jews into the Gentile population.

It is wrong to speak about the relationship of Christians and Jews a-historically and dogmatically on the basis of the New Testament, as if this relationship could be deduced theologically without regard to the concrete situation. This does not imply a historical relativising of anti-Judaism but a concretising of theology, which must renounce its claim to be supra-temporal. 'Theology after Auschwitz' is not, as many people think, the dissolving of theology into the *zeitgeist*, but the only way of putting theology forward today in a responsible way. The fundamental mistake of theological anti-Judaism is its understanding of theology, which holds aloof from everyday situations and 'politics'. I cannot say whether, if I were a Jewess at the end of the first century, I would have embraced the cause of the Jews or of the Christians. But as a Christian in the Federal Republic of Germany in 1984 I am obliged to say that the mass annihilation of Jews by my own people is something that still cries to heaven. I can give a historical explanation of Mark 3:6 and many similar NT texts and perhaps even relativise them; but as far as I am concerned they do not form part of the Gospel of Christ.

The fact that, for me, Christ is the Lord of the world and the Messiah of God does not mean that he wishes other peoples and cultures to be ruled, exploited and annihilated by Christians. These terrible things are also the result of an a-historical Christology which deduces its own claims to religious and political superiority from its confession of faith in Christ. Properly understood, the universal significance of Christ means, not that Christians regard their liberation by Christ as their private salvation, but that they believe in a Lord who desires the salvation and the liberation of all people. (Nor does this mean that all people and their religions are to be measured against the yardstick of Christian doctrine.) Even at the level of the macro-context of the synoptic gospels, the universality of the reign of God to which Christians look forward has no 'imperialistic' structure. God's reign over the world—illustrated in the tree of the world among whose branches the birds of the air find shelter (Mark 4:30–32 parr.)—puts an end to all domination of men over other men. And the evangelists did *not* say that all people must believe in Jesus as the Messiah if they are to receive God's salvation. What they said was that all people ought to learn to live according to the will of God. The decision is to be made at the practical level, not at the level of doctrine (see Matthew 25:31–46).

Without playing down the anti-Judaistic sentiments expressed in the gospels, we can ask whether it is really the case that NT Christology is 'essentially' anti-Judaistic. In my estimation this is only true of a Christian theology which claims doctrinal absoluteness and which therefore understands the NT in the same absolute terms. The *praxis* which is part and parcel of faith in Christ and hope in the sovereign reign of God is that of working to promote the life of God's creation. It is not something invented by Jesus or those who came after him: it follows from the Jewish faith in God, irrespective of belief in Christ, then as now. The story of the 'plucking of the ears of corn on the sabbath' is not the vehicle for theological anti-Judaism—not because it depicts Jesus non-Christologically, but because it draws its conclusions from the Torah in finding a *practical* solution to human need. Dialogue between Jews and Christians could result in Christian theology once more seeing faith and action as a unity—as in the NT. Here, judged by the Hebrew Bible *and* the New Testament, Christian theologians appear in a poor light.

2. PAUL AND THE LAW

In 1 Thess. 2:14–16 we have a clear expression of anti-Semitism, for here Paul not only speaks of 'the Jews' as the people of God subject to God's anger, he also slanders them politically: 'who . . . displease God and oppose all men . . .' In Paul's eyes the refusal of 'the' Jews to accept the mission to the Gentiles, which did not require circumcision, and the resultant persecution of Jewish followers of Jesus at the hands of Jews, justified the ancient world's anti-Semitic case against the Jews. But in producing this new justification for existing anti-Semitism Paul also paves the way for a persecution of Jews by Roman authorities, for they justified such persecution on the grounds of Jewish *'odium humani generis'*—hatred of the human race. It is inexcusable that Paul should have written these words, and uttered them, no doubt, all too often. The fact that he himself was once involved in the same kind of persecution of Christians, i.e., that he was a convert full of hatred for his own past, does not exonerate him. The accusation he makes against 'the Jews' was no doubt used later, under Nero, in the latter's persecution of the Christians. In Paul's lifetime, in the eyes of the Roman authorities, the persecution of Christians would have seemed to be like the persecution of Jews. In accusing 'the Jews' of enmity against all men Paul is portraying them as being disloyal to the Roman State. Taking 1 Thess. 2:15 together with the presentation of Jewish attitudes in Acts (see Acts 17:7), we must imagine that Jews and Jewish and non-Jewish Christians denounced each other, each delivering the others up to the Roman knife.

This same Paul earnestly grappled with the theological problem, that the Jews as a people have rejected faith in the Messiah, Jesus. It is impossible to harmonise 1 Thess. 2:14–17 with the Latter to the Romans (and incidentally Paul's ideas about women Christians cannot be harmonised either). As I see it we have no choice, theologically speaking, but to approach the NT, and hence Paul, just as we approach the issue of sexism (and slavery) and anti-Judaism. At the same time, the way Paul wrestles theologically with the rejection of Jesus the Messiah by Israel according to the flesh, and with the meaning of 'law' in the perspective of the Christian faith, is a central theological factor in clarifying the roots of Christian identity and the tools of Christian anti-Judaism.

In its own terms, Paul's 'doctrine' of justification is not an alternative teaching on law over against that of the Jews. Nowhere does Paul present opposing propositions or draw the borderline between himself and a Jewish concept of law. We only find this in the interpretations of Paul by Christian theologians of later times—including those of our own time. Paul bases himself on a doctrine of the Torah which is no different from that of Jewish teaching: '. . . doers of the law . . . will be justified'—by God (Rom. 2:13). Furthermore, the view that the only way to salvation is through the mercy of God, not works, is a theological principle which Paul shares with the tradition of post-biblical Judaism and the Hebrew Bible. It is the Christian anti-Judaism of later times and of contemporary theology which has deleted the central significance of the mercy of God from Jewish faith. In formulating antitheses such as Rom. 10:3 Paul is not comparing a divergent Jewish opinion with his own; he is interpreting the *attitude* of Jews who refuse to believe in Christ: 'For, being ignorant of the righteousness that comes from God . . . [they sought] to establish their own'. This does not mean that Jews said: 'We establish our own righteousness by keeping the Torah'; rather, Paul is saying that their rejection of faith in Jesus Christ is *de facto* the attempt to be righteous without God. They think they are serving God and receiving his salvation, but Paul says that without Christ they are in no position to serve God. Their doctrine is correct, but their attitude is wrong in that they reject faith in Christ.

Thus Paul is a pious Jew trying to convince other pious Jews that their whole approach to God is stiffnecked and illusory if they will not believe in Christ. They imagine that they can live according to God's will and keep the Torah; they do not believe Paul when he says that it is only possible to 'walk by the Spirit' (Gal. 5:25) if Christ's life-giving power is present. If we are looking for 'doctrinal' differences between Paul and his own people, we shall find them primarily in the evaluation of the power of sin, although here too Paul is not putting forward his doctrine against some other doctrine. For Paul the power of sin is that of a tyrant ruling the world. The sum of mankind's sinful deeds produces a system of collective compulsion which is all-embracing: all history since Adam is a history of sin. Indeed, even the Torah, God's holy, life-giving will (Rom. 7:12) is perverted by sin, so that God's good will becomes the instrument of death: 'For the law brings wrath', i.e., divine judgment (Rom 4:15). According to Paul the Jews fail to see the all-embracing power of sin. They do not notice the contradiction in their own practice, on the one hand teaching God's will to others in the belief that they are trusting in God, and on the other hand failing to keep the Torah themselves (Rom. 2:15–24).

Once Paul had accepted faith in Christ, he had to wrestle for the rest of his life with non-Christian Jews. This dispute was based on a different diagnosis of the human condition and on his belief that God, in the death and resurrection of Christ, had made it possible for men to have life, had broken the power of sin. Paul's view of sin as a universal power, far more significant than men's sinful acts, has a great deal to do with the conditions under which Jews (like other subject peoples) lived in the Roman Empire of the time. His battles with Jewish Christians on account of the circumcision of non-Jews were the result of this basic approach. He could not accept that non-Jews, eating and living together with Jews, should be circumcised, for it would be to restrict the saving significance of Christ. Jews and non-Jews are subjected by sin to the same oppressive system. They both have the same means of access to God's salvation: Christ. They both stand before the *one* God (Rom. 3:30). Since this God has given the People of Israel a special promise, Israel's present obstinacy, refusing to accept Christ, cannot be ultimate; in the end 'all Israel will be saved' (Rom. 11:26).

The conflict between Paul and his own people is based on his radical view of the power of sin and on his belief that this power of sin has been broken by Christ's death and resurrection. Apart from the above exception in 1 Thess. 1:15f., the conflict is set forth by Paul in the theological categories of the Jewish and biblical tradition. Paul does not want to replace a false or inferior theology with a better one; what he wants is to help proclaim God's already realised intervention in the history of sin, and to point men to the way which leads to life in a world which is enslaved to sin and death.

Seen in its historical context, the unconditional character of Pauline Christology can in no sense be called anti-Judaistic. Paul does not depreciate Judaism's religious significance vis-à-vis Christianity, nor does he dispute Israel's identity as the People of the Promise. One can go so far as to say that he wants all men to be Jews in the sense of Rom. 2:29 (albeit his definition of 'being a Jew' is different from that of non-Christian Jews). However, once Christianity came to see itself as a religion, distinct from the Jewish religion, the mere repetition of Pauline passages served to promote anti-Judaism on a massive scale. With regard to the present, from a theological point of view, this means that it is not enough to foster an awareness of actual anti-Judaism in the NT and later Christian theology; it is irresponsible simply to quote NT passages without providing them with a hermeneutics which reflects their social milieu. Such a hermeneutics must take account of the present reality of Christianity and Judaism and of their shared history. It must not limit itself to translating Pauline ideas; it must include Pauline praxis (under changed circumstances). Paul wanted to show all men the way to life which God had opened up; he did not want to disqualify other people from a religious point of view. If Christians today seek to live *their* commitment—their faith in Christ and their attempt to experience the love of God—to explain it and provide an example to others, no offence will be given to anyone else.

Properly understood, the unconditional nature of faith in Christ is something that belongs exclusively to prayer, worship, practical love and hope for the world. If it has even the slightest dealings with power-structures, it turns into an anti-Judaism and a cultural superiority-complex, to which whole nations are prone. This has been demonstrated by our own German history. Its wrongs cannot be softened by saying that the Nazis were anti-Christian—as if this somehow put Christians beyond reproach. The superiority-complex which makes use of Christology or its imitations is a definite part of the history of Christianity. Nowadays this has become unmistakable, at a time when genocide is again raising its head—conceived, supported and technologically perfected by Christians. Even today the fact that this is possible is connected with Christian anti-Judaism, which had put forward a Christology which claims superiority and disqualifies works, action and living according to scripture. In anti-Judaistic interpretations of Paul (e.g. that of R. Bultmann) we regularly find this denigration of deeds, of works, of actions according to the will of God: they are 'trusting in one's own strength', 'attempting to be autonomous', the 'drive for self-realisation', which are supposed to characterise the Jew—who here stands for all those who are on the wrong track. This is often summed up in the mere word 'law'. Thus Christians dispense themselves from the obligation actually to live according to God's will as it is found in scripture and interpreted by Jesus in the Sermon on the Mount.

3. JOHN AND THE JEWS

The Gospel of John is striking in its liberal use of the cliché 'the Jews', which here runs through the whole spectrum of values, from the straightforward designation of Jesus' membership of the Jewish people (as opposed to the Samaritans, 4:9), through the distancing evident in its referring to feasts 'of the Jews' (2:13 *passim*), right up to the negative usage, i.e., Jesus in conflict with fickle and irresolute groups among the people (e.g. 6:41), the Jewish leaders, 'Pharisees' and 'high priests', seen as the prime movers of the execution of Jesus (11:47). John's Gospel presupposes that Christians have been refused membership of the synagogue by the Jewish leadership (9:22; 12:42; 16:2). Christians experience this exclusion from the synagogue as this world's hatred (16:2 in context). We must conclude that it is *Jewish* Christians who are thus excluded. In presenting the path taken by Jesus this Gospel is simultaneously always describing the experiences of the Johannine communities around the time when the Gospel was written (after 70 A.D.). Employed as it is in this summary and often negative way, the term 'the Jews' is used by a minority within Jewry to express their bitterness at the treatment Jesus and his followers have received at the hands of their own people.

The picture of the situation of the Jewish people is a very nuanced one; here it is only seen in terms of the relationship of Jews to Jesus and his followers. The people have messianic expectations; they adopt a definite, critical approach to Jesus' messianism, as does he to theirs (see 6:15). There are secret followers of Jesus even among the 'rulers' (e.g. 3:1), but they lack courage (11:42 f.). Also, it was for fear of the Romans that some of the Jewish leaders persecuted Jesus and had him put to death. They were afraid of the political consequences if the Romans became aware of the increasing messianism among the people which Jesus inspired (11:48). So 'the Jews' distance themelves politically from Jesus and make an exaggerated profession of loyalty to the Emperor (19:15). The Gospel of John presents a one-sided, vivid and nuanced picture of the situation of the Jews after the destruction of the Temple. The nation has a leadership which even Rome recognises, but it is under great political pressure and cannot risk allowing a messianic movement to flourish around Jesus, even a 'messianic' movement with a king whose kingdom is not of this world (18:36). Even if this movement has no military power and no direct political aims, from the Roman point of view it is still part of that Jewish messianism which constitutes a threat. In the Gospel of John 'the Jews' and the followers of Jesus are both victims of Roman politics; here, Christians are an oppressed minority within a conquered, subject and harassed nation. To accuse the Jewish leadership as it is portrayed in John's Gospel of opportunism vis-à-vis the Romans, or to accuse the Christians, of whom this Gospel is an embodiment, of anti-Judaism, is to apply labels which are inappropriate to the historical situation. A more worthwhile insight would be this: people in oppressed nations may be under the heel of their overlords, but this does not automatically make them capable of solidarity, as we can see from 1 Thess. 2:15b.

So our earlier remarks about Paul also apply to the Gospel of John, i.e., unless properly translated into the terms of Christianity's new situation, the mere repetition of Johannine expressions will seem to indicate a theological anti-Judaism, which should longer count on naive or unprotesting acceptance.

Translated by Graham Harrison

Leonore Siegele-Wenschkewitz

The Contribution of Church History to a Post-Holocaust Theology: Christian Anti-Judaism as the Root of Anti-Semitism

THE DECISION of the Rhine Synod in January 1980 on renewing the relationship between Christians and Jews gave as the chief reason for the historical necessity for the Church to attain a new relationship to the Jewish people 'the awareness of the Christian share in the responsibility and guilt for the Holocaust, for the outlawing, persecution and murder of Jews in the Third Reich'.[1] That presents a comprehensive demand that has hardly been met as yet. What is it that stands in the way of awareness within the German theological world and the German Church of the Christian share of responsibility and guilt for the Holocaust?

At the end of the Second World War the *Confessing Church* in Germany was recognised by the Allies as a resistance organisation, and it was on this presupposition that the first studies were made of the history of the Evangelical Church in Nazi Germany. As a rule the historians had themselves been members of the Confessing Church, and they described their own history in the sense that, despite persecution by the Nazi régime, the Confessing Church had succeeded in keeping God's word loyally and giving the Church's prophetic witness. Admittedly, in the Stuttgart confession of guilt of 19 October 1945 the Council of the Evangelical Church in Germany had declared before representatives of other churches: 'We accuse ourselves of not having confessed more bravely, prayed more loyally, believed more cheerfully and loved more ardently.' But at the same time this statement said: 'Throughout long years we fought in the name of Jesus Christ against the spirit that found its terrifying expression in the Nazi rule of force.' The Confessing Church lived in the awareness that a clear antithesis existed between Nazism and Christianity, that in the *Kirchenkampf* the Confessing Church belonged to the victims of the Nazi régime.

At the start of the 1960s younger historians who had not been old enough to have played an active part in this struggle themselves turned their attention to groups within the Evangelical Church that had no ideological reservations about collaborating with Naziism and in practice did so. But against the background of German Christians who collaborated with Naziism the Confessing Church remained the true Church of Jesus Christ which had known and seized the hour when it was put to the test.

The *church's relationship and attitude to the Jews* was not a separate subject in these studies. People were aware that the German Christians had been prepared to make far-reaching compromises with regard to the Nazi philosophy, especially with regard to racism. But the Confessing Church was regarded as a model of integrity in view of its standing up for the Jews.

At the end of the 1960s three dissertations were presented which had as their subject the attitude of the Evangelical Church to the Jewish question, as it was called, during the Weimar Republic and in the Third Reich. These studies brought to light how great the failure even of the Confessing Church had been with regard to the Jews, and the way in which traditional anti-Jewish and anti-Semitic ways of thought had prevented even the Christians of the Confessing Church from speaking out and acting without compromise and unequivocally on behalf of the persecuted Jews. Although these historians broke the silence over the Jewish question, it is significant that their dissertations were not printed. Their attempts at a scholarly re-appraisal and investigation of the problem, attempts which could have stimulated a public debate among theologians and in the church, were thus nipped in the bud. Within the framework of the academic discipline of Church history the question of the relationship between Christians and Jews remained a subject that was taboo—and it still is.

Despite the fact that the Confessing Church saw itself in the way I have sketched out above, it was finally former members of that church who after a period of silence came together to launch an initiative at the level of the Evangelical Church in the German Federal Republic. In 1961, at the German Evangelical Church Congress, the Protestant lay movement, a *study-group of Jews and Christians was formed*. Here in a joint effort Jews and Christians made a start towards at least calling by its proper name a past that was so painful and so burdened with guilt in order to create the conditions for a renewal of the relationship between Christians and Jews. The way for Christians to give their relation to Jews a new shape by giving up their thousands of years of anti-Judaism had been shown by the Swiss Reformed theologian Karl Barth. Jews and Christians in Germany also received stimulation from Jewish and Christian theologians in America who had already begun on working on a post-Holocaust theology.

In this circle of the Jews and Christians who came together in the Kirchentag study group German-Jewish relations in recent German history emerged as the main subject. Study of the historical sources gradually led to the insight that what happened during the Nazi period in Germany had a long pre-history. Racial anti-Semitism had not fed merely on pagan and secular sources but could to a considerable extent build on the religious tradition of hostility towards Jews and blend into this. This shattering discovery was made by historical research: *religious hostility towards Jews was a central element of Christian theology from the start*. Anti-Judaism was and is an essential component of Christian theology inasmuch as Christian theology traditionally distinguishes between Christianity and Judaism with the aim of showing that there ought not to be any more Jews after Christ. To this extent anti-Semitism is a secular form of anti-Judaism.

On the basis of the frightening awareness that after the Holocaust there were hardly any Jews any more in Germany Christians have begun to re-think and re-shape their attitude to the Jews both theologically and in the life and practice of the Church. They become open to the biblical message that Christians and Jews are the one, even if divided, people of God; that the covenant which God entered into with his people Israel is not under notice of abrogation. Christians have begun to make themselves open to Jews' authentic understanding of themselves. It is ultimately a question of a new interpretation so that in all fields of theology and in all spheres of the Church's life the Holocaust is taken seriously and interpreted as the end of a theology directed against the Jews.[2]

Great interest was aroused in West Germany in the work of this study group, which approached the public through lectures, dialogues on biblical studies between Jews and

Christians, and publications. In the more than twenty years that it has been able to arouse a great number of Christian laity and clergy to re-think the relationship between Christianity and Judaism and to do so in a way that produces result in their immediate work: in preaching, in teaching, in their political attitude to the state of Israel. On the basis of the study group's work and initiatives, and on the basis of a proposal by the Rhine provincial synod in 1965, the Evangelical Church in Germany formed a study commission on the Church and Judaism at the start of the 1970s. With the help of Jews this produced a study of this question in 1975. The 1980 resolution of the Rhine synod, similarly drawn up with the help of Jewish theologians, also goes back to an initiative of this group.

Christian-Jewish history, the holocaust, Christian-Jewish dialogue, the attitude to the state of Israel of Christians and Churches have become questions occupying the Evangelical Churches in West Germany, but only to a lesser extent do they concern academic theology in this country.

The Protestant faculties of theology have a reserved and cautious attitude towards this complex of subjects. Hence a research gap has to be admitted with regard to the *history of the German faculties of theology in the Nazi period*. While in recent decades the churches have given details of their record, have been called publicly to account for their decisions and also their sins of omission, and have given an account of their doings, the theological faculties have not been drawn into this process of investigation, formation of opinion and self-examination. In fact it must be said that what is lacking is a precise picture of the theological faculty at that time, the work of faculty meetings, and of individual teachers inside and outside the faculty under the title 'Scholarship in the Third Reich'.[3]

The fact that the history of the theological faculties lies in shadow despite the lively and extensive historical writing about the Church's struggles during this period may be due to the faculties' ambiguous position between State and Church. While the work of teachers of theology at these faculties is related to the service of the Church, economically and legally they are civil servants and thus subject to the State's disciplinary regulations, something that was continually being impressed on them by the Nazi State.

On the other hand, within Protestantism the theological faculties share in the exercise of the teaching office. During the Nazi period the provincial churches and church groups repeatedly asked the faculties for expert reports on topical issues affecting theology and the church. It was for example in this way that the faculties of Marburg, Erlangen and Tübingen issued their statements on the validity within the church sphere of the regulations requiring people to carry identity cards showing that they were Aryan. The Leipzig faculty issued an expert opinion on the theology of the German Christians of Saxony: there are lists of signatures of German professors of theology on the questions of the New Testament and the race question and on Church confession and order. It is clear that even the Nazi State could not stop the theological faculties being involved in the Church struggle. But historical writing gives only a fragmentary reflection of this actual situation.

The decisive reason for this lack is the fact that the history of the faculties of theology during the Third Reich hardly redounds to the credit of the German theological progession. Even if individual academic theologians like Dietrich Bonhoeffer, Karl Barth, Hans von Soden and Rudolf Bultmann provided an important stimulus for the assertion of its claims by Christian theology and the Church, even if individual faculties like those at Bonn and Marburg tried to support the Confessing Church, nevertheless this handful of theologians and faculties is balanced by a much larger number who were concerned to achieve a frictionless and harmonious co-operation between Christianity and Naziism. It is necessary to realise that *the history of the faculties of theology in the Third Reich has to a considerable extent been a history of collaboration with Naziism*. The full extent of the co-operation that actually took place between Christian theologians and Naziism has not yet been perceived. Even during the Third Reich the Protestant faculties of theology had lost so much credibility among those attached to the Confessing Church that the latter set up its own seminaries with teachers it could trust.

The form taken by this collaboration between professors of theology and Naziism can be described briefly. The task theologians set themselves in the context of the racial anti-Semitism of the Nazi régime was to *'de-Judaise' theology and the Church and indeed Christianity as a whole.* Christinaity should be separated from its Jewish roots: people tried to rid themselves of the joint Judaeo-Christian tradition handed down in the Bible by stressing the aspect of mutual struggle and Christianity's assertion of its own identity vis-à-vis Judaism.

For this intellectual annihilation of the Jewish heritage within Christianity there were various State and Church institutions in which well-known theologians collaborated: the Reich Institute for the History of the New Germany, which was founded in Munich in 1936 under the direction of the Nazi historian Walter Frank and in which two Protestant professors of theology from Tübingen were trying to work out a concept of race for the history of ideas; the Bremen Bible School of the 'Church of the Future', which was set up by the city's German Christians and which wanted to produce a 'de-Judaised' Bible; and the Institute for the Investigation of Jewish Influence on German Church Life founded in Thuringia in 1939 on the Wartburg near Eisenach. These two Church institutions were able to include a large number of theologians in anti-Jewish study groups. There was hardly a single one of the eighteen state faculties of Protestant theology in Germany where at least one member of the staff, and usually several, were not involved in some State or Church programme of 'de-Judification'.

Because they regarded anti-Judaism as belonging essentially to Christianity, these theologians were not able to draw a boundary which would shut off racial anti-Semitism. The kinds of theological argument they used against Judaism took on an immediate political relevance in the conditions of the Third Reich: for example, their argument that the relationship of Christianity and Judaism was to be determined solely on the basis of the opposition between the two religions cut the Christian Churches off from the Jews; it released them from their responsibility for the Jews and indeed aimed at forging a coalition with the Nazis. It was asserted implicitly and explicitly that Naziism and Christianity were allied in the struggle against the Jews.

A further anti-Jewish argument that could easily merge into Nazi anti-Semitism was that Christianity went beyond Judaism and superseded it, that ethically it was the superior religion. This kind of theological thinking in terms of progress made Judaism inferior as a religion and, because it had been superseded by Christianity, superfluous. In Nazi propaganda the argument appeared as the superiority of the Aryan race over the inferior and immoral Jewish race.

The integration of anti-Jewish thinking and behaviour in anti-Semitic ideology and policies did not happen for the first time in Nazi Germany. On innumerable occasions in the history of the Church *anti-Jewish theological arguments have led to pogroms.* In previous studies I have tried to show this with the help of some striking examples: Luther, the Tübingen New Testament scholar Gerhard Kittel, and the 'people's theologian' and exegete Walter Grundmann.[4] But I cannot help asking whether theological anti-Judaism is simply a problem of German Protestantism alone and whether Catholic and non-German theologians are not equally affected by it.[5] This offers a wide field for critical investigation. From a structural point of view a theology that favours and endorses racism uses the same pattern of arguments as Protestant theologians did in order to join them in proceeding against the Jews of their time.

A theology that aids the intellectual and physical annihilation of the Jews and indeed of any supposed opponent betrays the Gospel of Jesus Christ. If Christians in Germany did not want to recognise this and could not recognise this before the Holocaust, after Auschwitz it has become an irrefutable insight. After Auschwitz we Christians have to turn and change our ways, so that we grasp the pernicious nature of any kind of hostility towards the Jews as a sin against the Holy Ghost.

Translated by Robert Nowell

Notes

1. *Zur Erneuerung des Verhältnisses von Christen und Juden*, Handreichung 39, (Düsseldorf 1980), p. 9.

2. *Auschwitz—Krise der christlichen Theologie*, ed. R. Rendtorff and E. Stegemann (Munich 1980).

3. There are some preliminary studies and investigations of individual cases, and these are examined in L. Siegele-Wenschkewitz 'Neutestamentliche Wissenschaft vor der Judenfrage' (*Theologische Existenz Heute 208*) (Munich 1980), p. 8: they have hardly been accepted by theological research in Germany. My own attempts at investigation have been taken up and discussed by foreign scholars: R. P. Ericksen 'Zur Auseinandersetzung mit und um Gerhard Kittels Antisemitismus', in *Evangelische Theologie* 43 (1983), 250–270; J. S. Vos 'Politiek en Exegese: Gerhard Kittels beeld van het jodendom' in *Verkenning en Bezinning* 17:2, 1983; and J. S. Vos 'Antijudaismus/Antisemitismus im theologischen Wörterbuch zum Neuen Testament' in *Nederlands Theologisch Tijdschrift* 38:2 (1983), 89–110.

4. L. Siegele-Wenschkewitz 'Mitverantwortung und Schuld der Christen am Holocaust' in *Evangelische Theologie* 42 (1982), 171–190, and 'Antijudaismus und Antisemitismus bei Luther' in *Martin Luther und die Juden: Die Juden und Martin Luther* ed. B. Klappert, H. Kremers and L. Siegele-Wenschkewitz (Neukirchen-Vluyn 1984).

5. The role of anti-Judaism as the foundation of anti-Semitism within Catholicism has been shown by the study by H. Greive *Theologie und Ideologie: Katholizismus und Judentum in Deutschland und Österreich 1918–1935* (Heidelberg 1969).

PART IV

Inter-disciplinary Reflections

Mary Knutsen

The Holocaust in Theology and Philosophy: The Question of Truth

IN AN important article entitled 'Christians and Jews After Auschwitz,' J. B. Metz addresses a clear imperative to contemporary Christian theologians: 'Never again to do theology in such a way that its construction remains unaffected, or could remain unaffected, by Auschwitz.'[1] And in the course of his own reflections on the implications of this imperative for contemporary Christian theology and Jewish-Christian dialogue, he issues the following warning about the question of truth. 'Everything has to be measured by Auschwitz,' he writes.

> This includes our Christian way of bringing into play *the question of truth....* But confronting the truth means first of all not avoiding the truth about Auschwitz, and ruthlessly unmasking the myths of self-exculpation and the mechanisms of trivialisation which have been so long disseminated among Christians.... Too often, in fact, has truth—or rather what Christians all too triumphantly and uncompassionately portrayed as truth—been used as a weapon, an instrument of torture and persecution against Jews.[2]

This essay begins by accepting the force both of that imperative and that warning. It thus takes on a particular double task: first to reflect on the meaning and implications of that imperative for contemporary Christian theology, and then, in and through that reflection, to raise once again the central question of truth, only now in a way that is deeply critical, that indeed is 'measured by Auschwitz'. For through this reflection, I hope also to suggest the need for a further extension of Christian theological thinking than has been generally acknowledged: the need to bring the question of ideology, and with it, the normative question of the conditions and criteria of non-ideological discourse, to the heart of Christian theological reflection on the truth of Christian religious and theological discourse itself.

1. THE SITUATION

'Never again to do theology in such a way that its construction remains unaffected, or could remain unaffected, by Auschwitz.' Already within this simple but extremely demanding imperative, it is possible to discern a certain sequence. First, and most importantly, there lies at the heart of this imperative an indicative, a statement of fact: Auschwitz has happened. Yet immediately this event is more than an event among other historical events, for it must divide theologies into a before and after; it is an *event that divides epochs*. At least part of the meaning of this imperative, then, is that Christian theologies acknowledge this and be affected by it. At the same time, however, it is a demand that Christian theological thinking be such that it can, in principle, recognise this and be open to alteration by this event; ruled out is not only any contemporary Christian theology that remains unaffected by Auschwitz but also any that 'could remain unaffected'. What kind of thinking need this be? What happens when it encounters the unalterable actuality of Auschwitz? It is this sequence and these questions which guide our reflection here.

We begin, as we must begin, with the indicative: Auschwitz has happened. It is not only the beginning, however it is also that to which we must constantly return and with which we will end. Indeed, the whole of this essay may be read as an attempt to explicate the interpretation of this fact which is already present in its first section. And yet we must begin here.

Lest this horrifying word 'Auschwitz' lose its historical concreteness, and with it, its horror, let us start by *stating the reality* it symbolises as badly as possible: the systematic torture and murder of millions upon millions of Jewish children, women and men has in fact occurred, carried out with relentless singleness of purpose, with the active or tacit complicity of untold thousands and the silence of the whole world, in the heart of the cultural, social and historical reality which is broadly Christian, European civilisation. In every country of Hitler's Europe, with the sole exceptions of Denmark and Finland, millions of human beings, from infants to the aged, were hunted down, often psychically and physically tortured, and killed, whose sole crime was that, as 'racially' defined Jews, they were still human beings, and alive. For those Jews living in countries under total, direct German rule there was no escape; ninety per cent were annihilated: 3 million Polish Jews, 228,000 from the Baltic countries, 210,000 from Germany and Austria, 80,000 from the Protectorate of Bohemia and Moravia, 1,352,000 from White Russia, the Ukraine and Russia. Other countries, too, yielded up the Jewish people to death: 105,000 from the Netherlands, 54,000 from Greece, 90,000 from France, thousands more from Slovakia, Hungary, Belgium, Yugoslavia, Rumania, Norway, Bulgaria, Italy, Luxembourg.[3]

The numbers, the geography of this death, stun. Yet with them we only begin our descent into the concrete actuality symbolised in the wold Auschwitz. Mind and imagination reel before the sheer scope of this machinery of dehumanisation and death, the horrifying numbers of those murdered and of those millions more, still silent, who actively or inactively acceded to its course; stagger at the bottomless depths of the hatred which is disclosed there, the unutterable evil for evil's sake of a human machinery which, superseding and even undermining military and political objectives, had as its sole purpose not only the imposition of death but also the extremest degradation and suffering prior to death; finally fall and shatter upon the unfathomable horror of the actuality: the infinite concrete detail, and the infinite unacceptability, of this human suffering and death. The harrowing, broken voices of the victims and survivors, the stories and images which must sear every still human imagination, the even more searing void of the thousands and thousands forever silent within them—these alone have the power, and the authority, to evoke the concrete actuality, the endless outrage of the reality symbolised in the word 'Auschwitz'. No philosophical or Christian triumphalism may be permitted here, no use of ready generalisations about the 'meaning' of such suffering, or the necessary 'moments' in history, or of having it all neatly 'covered' in Christian theological categories. All stand exposed before the terrible authority of those voices, before the overwhelming actuality and infinite unacceptability of this fact: Auschwitz has happened.

Yet already in this event, already more than an historical event among others, another indicative emerges: *Auschwitz qualifies and confronts us all*. It confronts us, first, as human beings, as persons still capable of feeling for, and dismay before, the sufferings of others. But it confronts us also as participants and heirs of the historical, cultural and religious world in which it occurred and which it has now unalterably altered and exposed. Participants in a cultural and historical world—religious, philosophical, political, social, cultural and linguistic traditions and histories—now irrevocably qualified by the fact that it has happened, and so faced with the necessity of understanding ourselves only in an historical world thus concretely qualified, none of us can go back 'behind' that event nor escape 'beyond' its irrevocable, unfathomable actuality. To understand at all, we can only do so in a history now broken open and traditions now exposed by the reality of Auschwitz. In this sense, it is not up to any of us to choose whether or not to confront the chasm in our history that is evoked in the word Auschwitz. Auschwitz confronts us—and it does so not just from afar but at the very centre of our historical, cultural and religious self-understanding.

Already at work here, of course, is not only an interpretive understanding of the event of Auschwitz but also an understanding of understanding, of reflection. This is our next set of questions, then. Since our imperative also rules out any Christian theology that 'could remain unaffected' by Auschwitz, what kind of thinking need this be? What happens when it encounters the actuality of Auschwitz?

2. THE HISTORICALISATION AND SOCIALISATION OF REFLECTION

Certainly the first, most immediately obvious requirement for such thought would seem to be this: Such thinking needs at least to be related to history and historical events, not just externally, as objects for a thought that understands itself in fixed, categorial terms and hence as outside of history, but internally, as capable of entering into the very conditions and 'affecting' the very course and construction of thought itself. It is this, I believe, that here lends particular significance to what might be called a new 'turn' in the understanding of the nature and tasks of human understanding evident in a number of different contemporary disciplines of thought, including the hermeneutic philosophy of H. G. Gadamer and the works of the Frankfurt School for Social Research from Horkheimer to Habermas. Despite the important differences between these works, and between the contemporary theologies that have been developed in conversation with them, there are also some even more important similarities: sustained critiques of monological, a-historical and dualistic models of thought and world and a recovery of an understanding of the social and historically changing constitution of the human world and of philosophy, social theory, and theology themselves as products of and participants in that ongoing 'social construction' of world.

It is clearly not possible, in the space of this essay, to begin to give a full interpretation of this 'turn', of any of the complex texts which diversely comprise it, or of its even more complex resonances with nineteenth century thought, and perhaps above all the works of Hegel.[4] Yet in order more clearly to specify some of its meaning and its implications for Christian theological thinking in a post-Holocaust world, I would like briefly to draw attention to the following four points.

First, there is at work here a deeply historical understanding of the dynamic and interactional character of human becoming. To put it as simply as possible, human beings are understood not as fixed 'natures' but as beings constantly in process of forming and transforming themselves thorough their technologically, socially and culturally mediated (and historically shaped and changing) interactions with each other and with the physical world.

A second point follows from the first: this formative interaction of human beings with each other and with the physical world is mediated (technologically, culturally, linguistically, etc.) and as such is bound up with *communicative interaction*, with language, and interpretation. Hence that self- and world-formative interaction has an intrinsically interpretive (hermeneutic) character; we interact with and come to understand each other and the world through continual acts of interpreting the (linguistic and extra-linguistic) media of that communicative interaction. Indeed, understanding itself can be understood as a kind of conversation with another requiring continual creative acts of translation— the generation of new 'languages'—through which alone we find and form an intersubjective and hence objective world.

Yet here a third point quickly follows: that communicative interaction is shaped by and conditioned upon the formative framework of linguistic, literary, cultural, social and religious traditions and institutions which themselves are products of a past and ongoing interaction between socially formed selves. There is no point 'outside' these traditions from which reflective thought may 'freely' survey and assess them; rather it can only understand and grasp in them the concrete conditions of its own possibility.

Yet—and this is the fourth and last point—as human agents capable of insight, creativity, reflection and action we are not just products of but also practical participants in this ongoing self- and world-formative process, capable of transforming, as well as being transformed by, our interaction with each other and so transforming as well the traditions and the institutions within which that interaction occurs.

In sum, as this series of points has been intended to illumine, the 'social-historical, hermeneutic and practical turn' in a number of contemporary disciplines, including theologies, may be understood to be founded on a recovery of an understanding of the social and historically changing constitution of the human world, and of philosophy, social theory and theology themselves as products of and practical participants in that ongoing social (or 'conversational' or communicative) construction of self and world.

What happens when a Christian theological thinking that understands itself in this way finds itself confronted with the actuality of Auschwitz? To put it more specifically: What happens to philosophical and theological reflection when history and society are understood not just as objects *for* but as constitutive *of* the reflective self? What new problems emerge at the interior of thought, challenging the very possibility of understanding or thinking at all? For my own part, these problems are at least two, and both emerge from an encounter with the actuality of Auschwitz: on the one hand, the irruptive force of historical events, and especially historical events of such enormity—of such radically unacceptable human suffering—that they shatter the traditional genres and even the very rhetoric of our historical (and religious) self-understanding; on the other hand the release of the (self-involving) question of ideological distortion in the traditions, texts and institutions in which one's own self-understanding has been formed—the systematic distortion in Christian traditions, teachings, and texts which is Christian anti-semitism. We turn then to a set of texts whose critical differences from the hermeneutic philosophy of H. G. Gadamer and others make an especially important difference for Christian theological thinking after Auschwitz: the work of the 'early' Frankfurt School (Benjamin, Adorno, Horkheimer) on the significance of historical events, and especially events of human suffering, for our historical (and religious) self-understanding, and the work of the 'later' Frankfurt School on the necessity and possibility of uncovering systematic distortions in the traditions and institutions which condition and shape our own understanding.

3. THE RUPTURE OF HISTORY AND THE RETRIEVAL OF APOCALYPTIC

Among the members of the early Frankfurt School, it is Walter Benjamin who has perhaps expressed most enduringly the significance of historical events, and especially events of human suffering, as a shattering of more cultural or developmental histories. The sense of the disparity between these is striking in Benjamin's work, most especially in the *Theses on the Philosophy of History*, completed in 1940, just before his death in flight from the Holocaust. 'The cultural treasures he surveys have an origin which he cannot contemplate without horror', he wrote. 'There is no document of civilization which is not at the same time a document of barbarism.'[5] Even more enduring is the imagery of the Angelus Novus, the angel of history who surveys the wreckage of history and would like to wake the dead and make whole what has been smashed but is blown by a storm from Paradise backwards into the future while the debris climbs skyward: 'This storm is what we call progress.'[6] In his 'fight for the oppressed past'[7] Benjamin thus rejects all historicist, cultural and universalist philosophies of history. Rather, his aim is 'to blast open the continuum of history'[8] both to disclose its wreckage and to leave it open to the dramatic, total break with history which is the messianic event, the redemption of the whole by an event and a power which Horkheimer would name only the Wholly Other.[9]   No other contemporary theologian is more imbued with the spirit of Benjamin's work and of this correlation between the unacceptability of human suffering, the rejection of developmental and evolutionary models of history, and the recovery of the apocalyptic than J. B. Metz. While his earlier work was marked by a concern to critique technocratic society and to recover the social-historical, practical and political within contemporary society and in Christianity, what has particularly marked his more recent work is his acknowledgment, with Benjamin, that what is encountered in that history—events of suffering and above all the event of Auschwitz—must explode any traditional historical narrative focused on the historical 'victors' and undo any teleological schema of history which would reduce the victims of history to a means to an end.[10] By contrast to the complacency, individualism and privatism of bourgeois Christianity, and by contrast to such models of history, Metz stresses the need for a narrative Christian theology in solidarity with victims which is I think deeply Markan: a narrative whose expression of and witness to particular negative events (remotely, the passion and death of Jesus and, more proximately, the destruction of Jerusalem) is at once made elliptical by the shattering negativity of those events and broken off by the apocalyptic expectation of the redemption of all which is imminent but still hidden, which is not yet.

Metz's theology has I think great power and importance as a critical corrective of every solely 'realised' Christian eschatology, as a powerful retrieval of the apocalyptic within Christian texts and traditions, and as an even more powerful expression of a response to human suffering and death which is at once deeply Christian, moral and rhetorical. First, it is a recovery, in contrast to what too often is a Christian complacency before the suffering of others, of a fundamental moral sensibility and principle. Within the framework of (personal) compassion for and (personal, political, and religious) solidarity with victims, there is also the necessity for the recognition of a double alterity: the otherness of the victim, whose experience of suffering and death may never be appropriated by another and whose testimony of that experience bears an inviolable authority;[11] and the otherness of that suffering and death from what should be. Thus it is a recovery, against what too often is a Christian complacency, of moral and human outrage, of shock and dismay before such suffering, an impassioned and Christian recognition that this should not be. At the same time, it is a recovery of the promise of the redemption of suffering and death and, with it, of the apocalyptic, the radically not-yet, in the Christian religious traditions. Indeed, I would like to suggest that each may work as a correlate and even cognitive condition for the other: the recognition of an event of human suffering of such enormity that it shatters every traditional theodicy and every traditional way of rendering such suffering meaningful and hence, finally, acceptable releases the recognition of the apocalyptic; to its character as an irruption which subscends both history and thought there is correlative a heightened awareness of its only possible redemption as an irruption which transcends the course of history and the categories of human thought. Conversely, the recognition of the apocalyptic can also be a condition of the recognition of the radical, permanently unacceptable character of that event, and indeed can enable a newly radical awareness of the totality of human suffering and death and of the totality of the redemption that is awaited. To hold together in a tensive, narrative unity this solidarity, this double alterity, and this expectation is I think the extraordinary power of the narrative Christian theology which Metz proposes; it is in many ways the extraordinary power of Mark.

Here then is I think a recovery of possibility for an authentically Christian response to the horror of Auschwitz which avoids the temptation both of Christian appropriationism and Christian complacency. That such a theology does not, and need not, replace but rather include a religious and theological understanding of such realities as the sheer giftedness of existence and the presence of grace to and in the world and in human life is I hope evident. To believe, as I do, that we also need speak of the gracious, redeeming presence of God in history is not, here, the statement of an objection; after Auschwitz it can only be the statement of a question, a question which I cannot answer and which in no wise is intended to lessen the importance of this response. In a post-Holocaust world, the recognition of the radical unacceptability of such suffering and of that radical not-yet might be an index not only of our Christianity but of our humanity as well.

4. THE RELEASE OF SUSPICION AND THE QUESTION OF TRUTH

It is a long journey from the religious and rhetorical power of that elliptical, broken narrative to the more theoretical requirements of ideology-critique, but it is a journey that must be made. Whatever qualification might be made about the Christian sources and character of Hitler's ideology, it is certain that the event of Auschwitz was shaped by and in multiple ways made possible by centuries and centuries of Christian anti-Semitism. Indeed, even apart from the complex historical and sociological tasks of uncovering causes and relationships—though these are important—it is not those but the event itself that makes this a moral and religious absolute: After Auschwitz, no form of Christian anti-Semitism can be tolerated. And it is that absolute which must release at once a *radical retrospective suspicion upon the Christian traditions*, texts, teachings and institutions and a *radical prospective suspicion* upon any assumed 'innocence' of Christian doctrines, symbols and narratives and their effects within the formative framework of the effective history of Christian anti-Semitism and contemporary religious, social and political institutions.[12] The task of ideology-critique here has not only to do with the past; it is, because we are shaped by that past, a present and prospective task as well.

Both the scope and the intensity of that suspicion have been evident in a number of important works published in the last ten years. In Rosemary Ruether's signal work, *Faith and Fratricide*,[13] it has included a critical uncovering of the roots of anti-Semitism in the New Testament (especially Matthew and John), in the traditions of interpretation in which those texts became further embedded in an even more systematic anti-Semitism, and in doctrines of Christ. This critical work has been extended as well as by other scholars into fuller examinations of the Pauline texts[14] and in the later traditions. Significantly, there has been wide agreement that a central feature of this developing anti-Semitism was the exclusivity of Christian rights to interpret the scriptures, and the corresponding development of the images of the Jewish people themselves as 'fleshly' 'carnal' and unable to recognise the 'spiritual sense' which are so ubiquitous in the Christian traditions. Christianity was the 'New Israel' superseding and replacing Judaism, which was then denied, explicitly or implicitly, any further right to continuing religious or human existence. That such a denial became horribly explicit in Auschwitz now renders even the implicit intolerable.

Equally evident in these writings has been the intensity of this suspicion: what is seen to be at stake is the very 'viability' of Christianity. Certainly a good part of this intensity stems from the moral and human horror of Auschwitz. But I would like to suggest as well that it has to do with an implicit operative understanding of the conditions of truth for Christian religious and theological discourse. Put most simply, and negatively, that condition is as follows: that no Christian theology, teaching, or symbol can be true which has the effect of systematically devaluing and denying the existence, authenticity, and rights to interpretation of others. Put more positively, it involves I think an important shift in the understanding of the character of religious and theological truth reflective of a recognition of the *communicative construction of self and world*: objectivity and truth are not a function of a monological correspondence of facts and theories but of a linguistically mediated intersubjectivity. What is at stake in a critique of the systematic distortion in Christian traditions, institutions and history which is anti-Semitism is not just the question of justice—the legitimation of oppression; what is also at stake as well is the question of truth—the question of whether Christian theologies and teachings and the institutional structures in which they are embedded do or do not enable a true, authentic and just community of interpretation and hence the intersubjective validation of its disclosiveness and truth within an unrestricted community of interpreters. It is this question that I think in different ways has also been brought in a number of other contemporary critiques of Christianity, again inner-Christian, even inner-Christian theological critiques: as reflecting and reinforcing sexism, racism, and classism. In the feminist critique of Christianity, for instance, a major focus has been not just on what the Christian traditions have said about women but also on the way in which its symbolics and teachings have, in determinate institutional and socio-political contexts, explicitly or implicitly effected the exclusion of women from the theological, religious, social, cultural and political 'conversation':[15] the question at issue has not just been that of the justice but of the truth of the understanding of word, self and God formulated in those contexts. In all of these critiques, in short, I think there is already operative an understanding of the conditions for a linguistically mediated intersubjectivity and consensus which Jürgen Habermas has developed in his theory of communicative competence. As such, his work can be a major resource, if critically corrected, for contemporary Christian theological reflection on the conditions of truth for Christian religious and theological discourse itself.

What is Habermas's theory of communicative competence? Though no full explication may be given here, we can note that he begins with a recognition of the communicative construction of self and world. In every communicative interaction with others, he argues, the intention of coming to an understanding (*Verständigung*) is already inherent. Because ordinary language communication has this inherent telos, a normative model of undistorted communication need not be imported from 'outside' ordinary discourse or history; it need only make explicit the norms implicit in our tacit understanding of what 'coming to an understanding' requires. As founded on an implicit understanding of what 'coming to an understanding' would be, Habermas argues that functioning language games are founded on an implicit underlying consensus about the criteria involved in distinguishing a true understanding or consensus (*Verständigung*) from a false one: a reciprocal recognition of not just one but four validity claims that speakers implicitly announce to one another in any communicative interaction. In addition to the claim to comprehensibility (that is, the competent use of linguistic rules in generating an intelligible utterance), he argues that ordinary language communication also rests on three additional validity claims for which all participants are tacitly expected to be responsible: (a) a claim to the truth of the propositional component of the utterance; (b) a claim to the truthfulness or authenticity of the speaker; and (c) a claim to the rightness of the norms of interaction and the appropriateness of the performatory component of the interaction to those norms. It is these norms, and Habermas's further explication of the entailments of their fulfilment, which I think can be a major critical and constructive resource for Christian theology.

To be sure, the resources in Habermas' work are also in need of critical correction. For my own part, a critique is particularly needed which will focus on what Thomas McCarthy has called the 'deemphasis of hermeneutic motifs'[16] in his work since 1970; what I would more strongly call a tendency to collapse the universal and transcendental structure and the hermeneutic, creative, and analogical realm of communicative interaction.

The development of formal criteria—of norms for non-ideological discourse—does not of course replace the task of uncovering the distortions in the traditions through the kind of critical interpretive work of Ruether and others; it is intended rather for its theoretical support and strength. Nor can it ever replace the level of our concrete, always metaphorical, always ambiguous attempts to understand ourselves, each other, and our world—and now in a way permanently qualified and affected by Auschwitz. We must return again to that beginning: Auschwitz has happened, and it confronts us all.

Notes

1. J. B. Metz *The Emerging Church* (New York 1981), p. 28.

2. *Ibid.*, pp. 21–22.

3. Data taken from Lucy Dawidowicz, *The War Against the Jews, 1933–1935* (New York 1975).

4. See Garbis Kortian *Metacritique* (Cambridge 1980) and the writings of Emil Fackenheim.

5. Walter Benjamin 'Theses on the Philosophy of History', and *Illuminations* ed. and introduced by Hannah Arendt (New York 1969), p. 256.

6. *Ibid.*, p. 258.

7. *Ibid.*, p. 263.

8. *Ibid.*, p. 262.

9. See Paul R. Mendes-Flohr 'To Brush History Against the Grain: The Eschatology of the Frankfurt School and Ernst Bloch' *JAAR* 51 No. 4 (December 1983) pp. 631 to 650

10. J. B. Metz *Theology of the World* (New York 1973) and Metz *Faith in History and Society* (New York 1980).

11. See Benjamin 'The Storyteller' in *Illumination*, p. 83–109.

12. See David Tracy *History, Historicity And Holocaust* from the Indiana University Converence on the Holocaust (Indiana University Press), forthcoming.

13. Rosemary Ruether *Faith and Fratricide* (New York 1974). See also for discussion of the work *Anti-Semitism and The Foundation of Christianity*, ed. A. Davies (New York 1979).

14. See E. G. Sanders *Paul and Palestinian Judaism* (Philadelphia 1977) and John Cager *The Origin of Anti-Semitism* (Oxford 1983).

15. See Mary Daly *Beyond God the Father* (Boston 1973).

16. Thomas McCarthy *The Critical Theory of Jürgen Habermas* (Cambridge, Mass. 1978), p. 379.

Mary Gerhart

Holocaust Writings: A Literary Genre?

IN THIS century there has been no greater challenge to the conventional understanding of literary genre than that brought to bear by Holocaust literature. The justification of this claim lies not only in the alteration of familiar genres by Holocaust writers and in their addition of new categories to the historical roster of literary genres; the justification is to be found also and more importantly in the ways in which Holocaust literature confronts and subverts our ordinary assumptions about the relationships between literature and history, literature and life, and the act of reading itself.

If we stay for a moment within the conventional notion of genre as category, the diversity of forms considered to belong to Holocaust literature is noteworthy. Besides book-length narrative accounts, and poetic expressions, it includes eye-witness accounts, heroic accounts of resistance leaders, last testaments, suicide notes, graffiti and fragments of sentences in hiding-places and execution chambers. Conventionally understood in terms of an historical era and its events—for example, in the ways some literature is said to be about the French Revolution and some is said to reflect the ideals and culture of the medieval world—we might expect Holocaust literature to be comprised of texts which are, like other literary texts, to be read eventually for topical interest, effectively distanced from the experiences which gave rise to them, and to be settled into genre types which unhesitatingly guide our reading of them.

However, literary texts which have as their major frame of reference the Holocaust seem less content than other historical fiction to be *about* the experiences of history—for example, of Buchenwald, Auschwitz, or the Warsaw ghetto. Instead, we find them expressing a double referent: first, a responsibility to tell what happened so that it will not happen again; and second, a fear of the domestication that possibly results when manifest violations of the human are converted into literature. By virtue of the tension between this responsibility and this fear, we will argue that Holocaust literature as a genre forces the reader to respond differently—to feel and to develop new habits of thought. In the words of Alvin Rosenfeld,

> Holocaust literature ... extends so far as to force us to contemplate what may be fundamental changes in our modes of perception and expression, our altered way of being-in-the-world. Just as we designate and give validity to such concepts as 'the Renaissance Mind' and 'Romantic Sensibility' and 'the Victorian Temper' to indicate earlier shifts in awareness and expression, so, too, should we begin to see that Holocaust literature is an attempt to express a new order of consciousness, a

recognisable shift in being. . . . Stunned by the awesomeness and pressure of event, the imagination comes to one of its periodic endings; undoubtedly, it also stands at the threshold of new and more difficult beginnings.[1]

Such descriptions give us a vivid sense of the radicality of the claims that are made about Holocaust literature. And so, one of the purposes of our genre analysis must be to ascertain if, how, and in what sense the foregoing claim is true. We will ask if Holocaust literature itself constitutes a genre as distinct from the discrete and conventional forms in which it is written (novels, diaries, poems, etc.). Finally, we will explore the significance of a genre analysis by asking if it provides any clues to critical and appropriate readings of Holocaust literature.

1. DOES HOLOCAUST LITERATURE CONSTITUTE A LITERARY GENRE?

Our first step will be to constitute the genre, and to do so we must begin with a redescription of some of its major forms. This description, according to the genre theorist Tzvetan Todorov, should be neither too particular nor too general.[2] In almost every general account of Holocaust literature, we find *diaries* mentioned first: specifically, *The Warsaw Diary of Chaim Kaplan*, Yitzhak Katznelson's *Vittel Diary*, Anne Frank's *Diary of a Young Girl*, Emmanuel Ringelbaum's compilation *Notes from the Warsaw Ghetto*, Mary Berg's *Warsaw Ghetto: A Diary*. Suppose that diaries are privileged texts in the corpus of Holocaust literature, not so much because they are most often written by victims rather than by survivors,[3] but because they raise, with special immediacy the question of whether or not the experiences of either victims or survivors are violated by being transformed into literature. Countless entries are punctuated with remarks to the effect that the author is either speechless in the face of the atrocities witnessed, or reluctant but driven to record events in language. In this hesitation, which runs through all of Holocaust literature, the status of literature in relation to experience is brought into question.

In the diaries, then, we find a leading thread to the constitution of Holocaust literature as a genre. The thread is *the issue of the adequacy of language*. On this issue, Holocaust literature is linked historically both to Jewish tradition and to other contemporary literature. In his introduction to Sidra DeKoven Ezrahi's poignant study of Holocaust literature, *By Words Alone*, Alfred Kazin recalls instances in the scriptures which manifest the Jewish sense of the limits of language: for example, the belief that the reality of God cannot be named and the notion that creation precedes and surpasses language. Ezrahi herself speaks of the 'economy of language' which prevailed in '*l'univers concentrationnaire*'—the economy of a 'self-contained world which both generated its own vocabulary and invested common language with new, sinister meanings'.[4] Quite apart from the dangers of speaking which existed in both the ghettos and the camps, parsimony of speech also became the condition for the possibility of new questions about destiny to be asked—questions which did not need to arise in ordinary times.

In the Jewish tradition, the reluctance to speak an event into language can be so strong that it imposes a dramatic or ritual banning of naming. In the Holocaust diaries this reluctance to speak proceeds not only from horror at the degradation of the human being but out of a disjunction of experience from credibility.

If diaries are privileged texts in Holocaust literature, *novels* best illustrate the range and scope of its imagination. According to Rosenfeld, some novels are explicit in their reference to the historical events, others transmute the events 'into more abstract visions of agony, absurdity, or mythic suffering',[5] and still others treat their subjects in a post-Holocaust state of mind. In Holocaust novels, the issue of the inadequacy of language is often represented by a mute, such as Jerzy Kosinski's The Boy in *The Painted Bird* and The

Silent One in Elie Wiesel's *The Town Beyond the Wall*. Mute characters play major roles in the plots of such novels, the major suspense of which is built on the discovery of the circumstances of the characters' 'going mute', and on the question of whether or not they will ever come to speak again.

In Wiesel's novel, for example, the character Michael has been incarcerated for interrogation and between the torture sessions he struggles to make one of his cellmates respond. 'This boy has a past; will I ever know about it? . . .' Relentlessly [Michael] persevered. The means at his disposal were poor. . . . 'I have nothing? No matter. I can push back the night with my bare hands. . . .' As soon as he was sure the boy was seeing him, he became a changed man. To set the boy an example he danced, laughed, clapped hands, scratched himself with his dirty nails, made faces, stuck out his tongue: he had to show the boy that being a man meant all this.[6]

Shortly Michael says to The Silent One: 'I know, little one: it isn't easy to live always under a question mark. But who says that the essential question has an answer? The essence of man is to be a question, and the essence of the question is to be without answer.' Michael plants ideas and values in The Silent One without having the satisfaction of hearing him speak before Michael dies. But Michael himself has been changed in the attempt, and the whole action of the novel denies that the efforts have been futile.

Holocaust narrative is best seen as simultaneous and parallel to the 'new literature', the general characteristics of which are the absurd, the disintegration of values, psychic discontinuity, and moral and physical atrocity. Language is also an explicit issue in the 'new' literature. In Samuel Beckett's *Stories and Texts for Nothing*, the narrator says in conclusion to one story, 'The memory came faint and cold of the story I might have told, a story in the likeness of my life, I mean without the courage to end or the strength to go on'. In Beckett's work, which reflects the pathos of Holocaust literature,[7] the issue of language is identified with the issue of literature, i.e., with the possibility of 'storying'. In other writers of new fiction, language is fashioned to reflect on language. In John Barth's *Lost in the Funhouse*, narrators comment on what heard words really mean, quotations of quotations are themselves quoted several times removed, a tape recording narrates its own story. In Robbe-Grillet's novels, simple words like 'fact' and 'see' are often in quotation marks as if to question either their meaning or their suitability. In literature like that of Barth, Beckett, and Robbe-Grillet, the issue of the adequacy of language appears most explicitly as meta-language—the use of language to call attention to language as language. Some German authors, too (Gunter Grass, Peter Weiss, Heinrich Boll, et al., who called themselves Gruppe 47) publicly recognised after World War II that the German language had been so inflated and distorted with Nazi Socialist propaganda that their first task was to restore the integrity of language. Holocaust poets, such as Paul Celan and Nelly Sachs, intensified the focus on language in their struggle with a 'silent' God. Despite the distinctiveness of their treatment of the issue of the adequacy of language, all of these texts attest to the centrality of the issue of language.

Does Holocaust literature, as a whole, constitute a genre? Or is it the case that there exists merely a thematic resemblance, spread over several, easily identifiable genres—the diary, the short story, the novel, the poem? There are at least three reasons for understanding Holocaust literature as a genre.

(a) Not only in diverse forms, but as a body of texts, the literature of the Holocaust challenges the very assumptions of literature in general. These assumptions are based primarily in the humanistic tradition which itself has undergone systematic criticism of its premises in the last decade.[8] Humanists assume that the function of literature in general is appropriately understood as catharsis (Aristotle), sublimity and beauty (Longinus), the suspension of disbelief (Coleridge), emotion recollected in tranquillity (Wordsworth)—

definitions which all tend to support a view of literature as an unqualifiedly constructive act of the imagination. Holocaust literature wavers in its self-understanding on this point, however; in its fidelity to the sinister acts of destruction which are its material object of attention, it is ambivalent in giving clues how it is to be best read. Perhaps it is incompatible to present the first Auschwitz as it was—a possible improbability—in such a way that a second Auschwitz becomes an impossible probability. This irresolution within the texts themselves results in a contradiction that is not contained by any humanist view.

(b) Since Holocaust literature has its roots in history of the twentieth century, one of its most distinguishing features is the way it calls into question the self-understanding of Judaism and of other related religious traditions. The predominant motif of traditional religious literature is that of heroic victory—over one's enemies, over adversity, over evil. Holocaust literature is modern literature: gone is the triumphalism which was the traditional perogative of being a survivor.

But perhaps the greatest unresolved tension in Holocaust literature is that it is both Jewish and contemporary. Read against the story in Maccabees of the woman and her seven sons killed by the king for refusing to eat ritually proscribed food, Holocaust literature manifests poignant similarities and differences. In 2 Maccabees 7, the brave victims of racism, one by one, go gallantly to their grisly deaths, singing and praising God for the privilege of dying by human hands in order that God's wrath against their nation might cease. In Holocaust literature, such unqualified acceptance—of God's wrath, of racism, of hope for the future—is gone forever. In pre-Holocaust history it had been acceptable to die for one's faith because doing so was a matter of choosing to do so. But the Holocaust deprived victims of choice, and so Jewish self-understanding was shaken: for the first time God seemed to have broken the Covenant. Without the Covenant, there were no Jews. Nor was there Yaweh. In the words of Paul Ricoeur, 'something has been lost, irremediably lost: immediacy of belief'.[9] This negativity is the meridian of our day.

Yet in this loss we perceive also a gain—a gain which is clearly one in authenticity and integrity for both God and humans. That this gain is also tentative and precarious is evident in the legend that concludes Elie Wiesel's *The Town Beyond the Wall*:

> One day man spoke to God in this wise: 'Let us change about. You be man, and I will be God. For only one second.'
> God smiled gently and asked him, 'Aren't you afraid?'
> 'No, and you?'
> 'Yes, I am,' God said.
> Nevertheless he granted man's desire. He became a man, and the man took his place and immediately availed himself of his omnipotence: he refused to revert to his previous state. So neither God nor man was ever again what he seemed to be.
> Years passed, perhaps eternities. And suddenly the drama quickened. The past for one, and the present for the other, were too heavy to be borne.
> As the liberation of the one was bound to the liberation of the other, they renewed the ancient dialogue whose echoes come to us in the night, charged with hatred, with remorse, and most of all, with infinite yearning.[10]

In this representative passage, we see a central belief of the tradition simultaneously retrieved and changed by being reformulated.

(c) To consider Holocaust writings as a genre is to reencounter the dilemma faced by the authors of that literature when they found that it was impossible to write and impossible not to write: merely to categorize texts *as literature* is to risk domesticating the originating experience. Whatever our theoretical reasons for reconstructing the notion of genre beyond the act of categorisation, Holocaust literature demands on principle that we do so.

2. THE SIGNIFICANCE OF HOLOCAUST LITERATURE

Even before that task is completed, however, Holocaust literature conceived as a genre suggests certain long-range effects of the reading of those texts, particularly in their treatment of human death. For whereas mortality is a fate common to all humans, that of the individual ('my' death) is phenomenologically a unique event. This understanding we have learned conceptually from Heidegger and this we reexperience in Holocaust literature as it re-presents both individuals and a people *in extremis*. Heidegger, however, emphasised the profundity of being-toward-death for human being. Holocaust literature by contrast represents a world in which mortality is made to appear cheap. By means of images of degradation, the reader of Holocaust literature is forced to enlarge the list of possible kinds of death and to relinquish any naive certainty about the forms of human mortality.

All of the great religions, without exception, face serious questions from within and without. Their uncritical assumption of patriarchalism, their literalism pertaining especially to the circumstances of their origins, their being oblivious to the injustices they themselves perpetrate on their own members—all these blindnesses make them particularly susceptible to the temptation to conceive of themselves as immortal. Holocaust literature conceived as a genre is strong evidence that one of the great traditions has come face to face with some of these questions and with its own mortality. In so doing, it provides a corrective to the vision of us all.

Notes

1. Alvin H. Rosenfeld *A Double Dying: Reflections on Holocaust Literature* (Bloomington and London 1980), pp. 60–61. See also Lucy Dawidowicz *A Holocaust Reader* (New York 1976), 'Introduction'.

2. Tzvetan Todorov *The Fantastic: A Structural Approach to Literary Genre* (New York 1973).

3. Diaries are often regarded to be privileged texts because they were usually composed by victims rather than by survivors. In doing a genre analysis of texts, however, privilege pertaining to the author must be suspended unless the texts themselves are affected. Moreover, not all diaries were written by victims nor even by eye-witnesses. Several survivors who recorded their reponses several years after the events are thought to have chosen the diary form in order to achieve a greater realism: the diary is a ready vehicle for vivid description and realistic documentation of facts. Nor does the diary require that the diarist draw relationships among phenomena which have no apparent connection or logic.

4. Sidra DeKoven Ezrahi *By Words Alone* (Chicago 1980), pp. x–xi, 10)

5. Rosenfeld, p. 71.

6. Elie Wiesel *The Town Beyond the Wall* (New York 1964), p. 174.

7. Charlotte Beradt *The Third Reich of Dreams* (Chicago 1968) quoted in Lawrence L. Langer *The Holocaust and the Literary Imagination* (New Haven and London 1975), pp. 45–46, 144–45.

8. See, for example, George Steiner's *In Bluebeard's Castle: Some Notes Toward the Redefinition of Culture* (New Haven and London 1971).

9. Paul Ricoeur *The Symbolism of Evil* (Boston 1967).

10. Wiesel, p. 179.

PART V

Editorial Reflections

Elisabeth Schüssler Fiorenza

David Tracy

The Holocaust as Interruption and the Christian Return Into History

1. FROM HISTORICAL CONSCIOUSNESS TO HISTORY

IN THE early modern period, the major historical events for new forms of Christian theology (liberal and modernist) were those two linked intellectual and historical explosions: the eighteenth century Enlightenment and the nineteenth century rise of historical consciousness. These events were clearly historical events in the usual sense of the emergence of new groupings of power, new institutions, and new concrete struggles. Nevertheless both events lent themselves more readily than the historical events of the twentieth century to a seemingly more intellectual even 'academic' set of theological questions. Perhaps the deceptively ahistorical character that many intellectuals accorded these events tempted Christian theology in that liberal period to focus its intentions less on concrete history and more on the seemingly ahistorical crisis of cognitive claims in Christian self-understanding (and especially the crisis of historical claims occasioned by critiques of the Enlightenment and the rise of historical consciousness). The theological major shift of interest in the last two centuries to the symbol of 'revelation' as the major symbol for theological attention is merely the clearest illustration of the kind of sea-change which occurred.

Indeed, as such atypical theologians in that period as Soren Kierkegaard saw, Christianity was in danger of becoming so exclusively a religion of cognitive 'revelation' that its function as primarily of religion of concrete 'salvation' could seem in doubt. This problem of a liberal retreat from concrete history was compounded by the fact that liberal optimism on cognitive meaning (and hence revelation) yielded theologies of salvation which functioned largely as theologies of triumphant intellectual reconciliation. The tragic irony soon became apparent: the very discovery of historical consciousness and the attendant theological furor with the crisis of the 'cognitive' claims tempted theology to retreat from history itself. It was Hegel's dialectical optimism, not his observation that history was a slaughter-bench, that largely won the liberal day. The gains of the historico-critical method and the classic liberal and modernist theologies which they occasioned are plain for all to see. But the loss—the loss of concrete history itself under the paradoxical cover of 'historical consciousness'—was a loss whose full impact we are just beginning to realise.

It is true that neo-orthodox theology—here understood as a self-critical moment within the liberal tradition—did correct the liberals at several crucial points. Above all, Karl Barth's rediscovery of the 'strange, new world of the Bible' can now be seen for what it was: a hermeneutic rediscovery of the fact that the subject-matter—the strange new world of the Christ-event to which all theology, including the scriptures, witnesses—must control all theological interpretation. This theological rediscovery was itself occasioned, as is well known, by the shattering impact of the First World War on earlier liberal optimism and self-confidence.

And what the neo-orthodox learned must still be honoured: the recognition of radical *historicity* beyond all liberal and optimistic senses of historical consciousness; the recognition that, theologically, the subject-matter of the eschatological event must rule; the recognition that this subject-matter forces a rediscovery of the need for *Sach-Kritik* in the scriptures themselves. The most enduring aspect of Bultmann's demythologising programme, for example, was not his concern with the cognitive dilemmas that modernity posed for Christian self-understanding (that we already learned from the liberals and modernists). His greatest contribution was his insistence that the eschatological *event* to which the scriptures witness enforces—within the scriptures and upon all later interpreters—a radical demythologising. What was said now must be judged critically by what was truly meant.

And yet even those characteristically neo-orthodox moves rarely brought Christian theology into concrete history. Rather the vertical transcendence of the neo-orthodox understanding of the eschatological event encouraged a theology increasingly privatised and thereby increasingly remote from the slaughter bench of history itself. For no less than the liberals, the neo-orthodox theologians often entered history a-theologically. Where the very discovery of historical consciousness paradoxically impeded the liberals' entry into history, radical historicity and the hermeneutic rediscovery of the absolutely transcendent character of the eschatological event paradoxically impeded a neo-orthodox entry into history—including, on the question of the Jewish people in Nazi Germany.

Karl Barth stated clearly in 1966 'We do not wish to forget that there is ultimately only one really central ecumenical question: that is our relationship to Judaism.' As profound as that statement is on christian theological grounds, it must still be asked: But what can this mean when that overwhelming historical event of our modern age—the Holocaust— is not accorded any theological weight?

What can it mean when this interruption in and to our history occurs? What can it mean for humanist liberal theologians and neo-orthodox Christian theologians alike when the history they theologically ignore crashes against itself in the horror of the Holocaust? Is there to be no *Sach-Kritik* here—and here alone? Is the question of Judaism—stated as *the* ecumenical question—a question to be divorced from the fate of the reality empowering all Jewish thought—the Jewish people?

Christian theologians of the modern period have honestly come to terms with historical consciousness and historicity on the unsettling events of the eighteenth and nineteenth centuries. They have developed a theological hermeneutics where the subject-matter—the event itself—is once again allowed to rule in theological hermeneutic. They have recognized the *Sach-Kritik* that the eschatological event itself demands. But they have too seldom returned to history—the real, concrete thing where events like the Holocaust have happened.

There is, in contemporary Christian theology, one great exception to these observations: the political, the feminist, and the liberation theologies. For behind the deprivatising demands of these theologies and behind their insistence on the priority of praxis over theory, behind their retrieval of the great suspicions lurking in half-forgotten, even repressed eschatological symbols, lies their single-minded and constant refrain: Christian theology must move past both liberal historical consciousness and neo-orthodox hermeneutical historicity and move again—as theology—into the concrete history of suffering and oppression. These theologies do not mean by history theories of historiography nor philosophies of history. They do not mean a purely vertical transcendence where history becomes a tangent, a theological accident. They mean history: they mean the concrete struggles of groups, societies, persons, victims, who have been shunted aside from the official story of triumph. They mean that the central theological question today is not the question of the non-believer but the question of the non-person—those forgotten ones, living and dead, whose struggle and memory *is* our history.

It is the singular achievement of these feminist, liberation and political theologians that their theological return into history—more exactly into the history of those whom official historical accounts including Christian theological accounts have disowned as non-persons, non-groups, non-history—has empowered these new theologies. As theologies they retrieve in and through their very suspicions the repressed interpretations of the New Testament such as the profound negations in the genre of apocalyptic—so embarrassing to the liberals, so unnecessary to neo-orthodox eschatologies.

Central in these theologies is the retrieval of the sense of history as interruption, as rupture, break, discontinuity in apocalyptic, the retrieval of liberation over easy announcements of reconciliation, the retrieval of the social systemic expression of sin over individual sins, the retrieval of the concrete praxis of discipleship. Given all this, there is yet more urgency for all theology to face the interruption of the Holocaust. For is it possible for any of us to insist upon the need for a Christian theological return to concrete history yet not face that? And if Christian theologians do face that historical *caesura*, can any of us any longer easily retrieve the 'fulfilment' theme always in danger of becoming a supercessionist theme, the lack of theological anger at Matthew 25 or the use of 'the Jews' in John's gospel, the uninterrupted use of traditional law-gospel motifs?

If Christian theology is to enter history, then surely this interruption of the Holocaust is a frightening disclosure of the real history within which we have lived. The theological fact is that Christian theology cannot fully return to history until it faces the Holocaust. It cannot face that interruption in history without facing as well the anti-Semitic effects of its own Christian history. It cannot face that interruption without realising that the return to history must now be the return through the radical negativity disclosed by that event. All the retrievals of those authoritative and formerly repressed themes which empower a theological return must yield to the radical *Sach-Kritik* which the eschatological event itself demands. Every hermeneutics of retrieval for Christian theology must today include a radical hermeneutics of suspicion on the whole of Christian history.

2. HISTORY IS CONCRETE

In 'Notes Toward Finding the Right Question' the Jewish writer Cynthia Ozick urges us to agree on three obligatory premisses when speaking about the Holocaust or in her words 'the European cataclysm': First, that it has no analogies, second that it is not a metaphor or 'like' anything else, and third, that it is not to be 'used' but only to be 'understood'. It generates 'lessons' to be learned or 'legacies' to be lived but it must not be 'used' in a partisan argument or polemical debate.

The legacy and lesson that Cynthia Ozick hears in its mournful language is that of 'having lost so much and so many'. What was lost in the cataclysm was not only the Jewish past but also its future.

We will never be in possession of the Novels Anne Frank did not live to write. It was not only the intellect of a people in its prime that was excised, but the treasure of a people in its potential. [In *On Being a Jewish Feminist. A Reader* ed. S. Heschel (New York 1983) pp. 120–151, at p. 134].

In order to comprehend the dimensions not only of Jewish loss but also of all of our loss more fully we have to 'understand' and articulate concretely the 'heart of Nazism' that generated such incomprehensible suffering and dehumanisation. The dehumanisation and suffering of the Holocaust may not become a theological metaphor for all human suffering but must be named in its political particularity. The ideological heart of Nazi-fascism was racism, its ideological catch-word was '*Untermensch*', the less than human, the sub-human being.

The genetic 'purity' of the Aryan race demanded the elimination of all those who could biologically contaminate it. The German '*Volkskörper*', German blood and German honour required not just the eugenic extermination of other 'subhuman' races (Jews, Gypsies, East European, or 'negroid' persons) but also the sterilisation and elimination of '*Entarteter*', asocial German women (unwed, promiscuous mothers, prostitutes, homosexuals, women in racially mixed relationships). The National-Socialist combination of racism and sexism moreover demanded strict sexual control of pure Aryan women, who were used as 'breeders' of the superior race. (The same was not true for German men who had licence to rape and abuse women of '*mindervertiger*' races). True German women were supposed to be 'handmaidens and servants', while '*Geschlechtsdemokratie*'—the democratic equality of the sexes—was labelled as 'Jewish' and 'communist'. (For documentation and analysis see *Frauen unterm Hakenkreuz* (Berlin 1983).

This combination of racism, sexism, and crude biologism in National-Socialist ideology proves it to be an extreme form of Western capitalist patriarchy that has found its classic formulation in Aristotelian philosophy and is historically mediated through Christian theology. In order to justify the exclusion of freeborn women and slaves from full citizenship Aristotle argues that their 'natures' are different and inferior to that of freeborn propertied men. Because of their 'subhuman' natures they must be kept in a state of submission and obedience, if the order and well-being of the State is not to be jeopardized.

In a similar fashion Christian theology has legitimated the different 'natures' and therefore inferior status of women and (until the last century) of slaves or 'native' peoples. Since the Enlightenment modern Western bourgeois society also was forced to develop an ideology that would justify the injustices of colonialism and imperialism on anthropological grounds. Genetic research, evolutionary theories, philosophical teachings, theological doctrines, all maintained that the European male citizen represents the highest human development (see W. Lepenius, *Soziologische Anthropologie* (Munich 1971) p. 73). 'Religious enmity' and biological-theological legitimisation of the 'subhumanity' of other races and women in capitalist patriarchy are the twin-roots of the 'European cataclysm'.

After having 'understood' and 'named' the forces of 'dehumanisation' that generated the unspeakable sufferings of the Holocaust we must draw specific 'lessons' and articulate the concrete 'legacies' of it. Christian biblical theology must recognise that its articulation of anti-Judaism in the NT goes hand in hand with its gradual adaptation to Greco-Roman patriarchal society. Christian as well as Jewish theology must cease to proclaim a God made in the image and likeness of Man. It can do so only when it mourns the 'loss' of women's contributions in the past and present and rejects our theological 'dehumanisation'. Moreover, white Christian and Jewish theology must promote the full humanity of all non-Western peoples and at the same time struggle against racism wherever it is at work. In short the memory of the Holocaust must 'interrupt' all forms of Western patriarchal theology if the legacies of the dead are not to be in vain.

Contributors

GREGORY BAUM was born in Berlin in 1923 and has lived in Canada since 1940. He pursued his studies at McMaster University in Hamilton, Canada, Ohio State University, USA, Fribourg University, Switzerland and at the New School for Social Research in New York. He is a Master of Arts and a Doctor of Theology, and is professor of theology and sociology at St Michael's College, Toronto University. He is editor of *The Ecumenist* and his publications include *Man Becoming* (1970), *New Horizon* (1973), *Religion and Alienation* (1975), *The Social Imperative* (1978) and *Catholics and Canadian Socialism* (1980).

REBECCA CHOPP teaches at the University of Chicago Divinity School. She received a Ph.D. from the University of Chicago in 1983, and her master's degree from Saint Paul School of Theology in 1977. Ms. Chopp works in the area of contemporary theology with a special emphasis in new forms of systematic thought.

ARTHUR A. COHEN is a theologian, cultural critic, and novelist. His work includes theological studies: *The Natural and the Supernatural Jew, The Myth of the Judeo-Christian Tradition* and the recent study *The Tremendum: A Theological Interpretation of the Holocaust.* His novels include *In The Days of Simon Stern, A Hero in his Time, Acts of Theft* and *An Admirable Woman.* A resident of New York City, he is a frequent contributor to many journals and he is also a lecturer.

ELISABETH SCHUSSLER FIORENZA has a licentiate in pastoral theology and a doctorate in new Testament Studies. She is currently professor of theology and NT Studies at the University of Notre Dame, Indiana. She has published numerous books and articles on new Testament Studies and Feminist Theology. She is active in the women's liberation movement in the Church and the academy and has served on various Task Forces on 'Women in the Church', 'Women in the Bible', or 'Women in Theology'. She was a member of the Core Commission of the Women's Ordination Conference, and together with Prof. Dr Judith Plaskow is the founding editor of the *Journal of Feminist Studies in Religion.* Her most recent book is *In Memory of Her. A Feminist Theological Reconstruction of Christian Origins* (New York)

MARY GERHART is professor of religious studies at Hobart & William Smith Colleges at Geneva, New York. She has an M.A. in literature from the University of Missouri and a doctorate in theology and literature from the University of Chicago. Her publications include *The Question of Belief in Literary Criticism: An Introduction to the Hermeneutical Theory of Paul Ricoeur* (1978) and *Metaphoric Process: The Creation of Scientific and Religious Understanding* (co-authored, 1984), and several articles. Her current work is on genre theory. She is editorial chair of *Religious Studies Review* and writes a bi-monthly book review column in *Commonweal.*

MARY KNUTSEN works principally in contemporary Christian theology. Her work includes discussion of hermeneutical theory, ideology-critique and feminist theory. She presently resides in Houston (Texas) and is teaching (summer 1984) in St John's University (Collegeville, Minnesota).

JOHANN-BAPTIST METZ was born in 1928 in Welluck bei Auerbach, in Bavaria, Germany, and ordained to the priesthood in 1954. He studied at the universities of Innsbruck and München, is a Doctor of Philosophy and Theology, and is professor of fundamental theology at the University of Münster as well as in charge of foundational studies for the University of Bielefeld. His publications include *Theology in the World* (1969), *Followers of Christ: The Religious Life and the Church* (1978), *Faith in History and Society: Towards a Practical Fundamental Theology* (1980), *Emergent Church: Future of Christianity in a Postbourgeois World* (1981).

JOHN T. PAWLIKOWSKI, OSM is professor of theology at the Catholic Theological Union (Chicago Cluster of Theological Schools), Chicago, Ill. (USA). He is the author of several books on the Jewish-Christian dialogue, the most recent of which is *Christ in the Light of the Christian-Jewish Dialogue*.

LUISE SCHOTTROFF was born in Berlin in 1934. She is married, with one child. Since 1969 she has been professor of new testament in Mainz. Her publications include: *Der Glaubende und die feindliche Welt. Beobachtungen zum gnostischen Dualismus und seiner Bedeutung für Paulus und das Johannesevangelium* (1970); with W. Stegemann: *Jesus von Nazareth, Hoffnung der Armen* (1978, translated into Spanish 1981, Dutch 1982); *Der Sieg des Lebens. Biblische Traditionen einer Friedenspraxis* (1982); 'Die Schreckensherrschaft der Sünde und die Befreiung durch Christus nach dem Römerbrief des Paulus' in *Evangelische Theologie* 39 (1979) 497–510; with W. Stegemann: 'Der Sabbat ist um des Menschen willen da' in *Der Gott der kleinen Leute* ed. L. Schottroff & W. Stegemann (1979) II pp. 58–70; ' "Mein Reich ist nicht von dieser Welt". Der johanneische Messianismus' in *Gnosis und Politik* ed. J. Taubes (1984).

SUSAN SHAPIRO received her Ph.D. at the University of Chicago from the Committee on the Analysis of Ideas and the Study of Methods. She is currently assistant professor in the Department of Religion at Syracuse University, where her work centres on Jewish philosophy and theology, hermeneutics, critical theory and rhetorical criticism. At present, she is completing a book on post-Holocaust Jewish Theology and hermeneutics as well as several articles in rhetoric and religion.

DAVID TRACY was born in 1939 in Yonkers, New York. He is a priest of the diocese of Bridgeport, Connecticut, and a doctor of theology of the Gregorian University, Rome. He is professor of philosophical theology at the Divinity School of Chicago University. He is the author of *The Achievement of Bernard Lonergan* (1970), *Blessed Rage for Order: New Pluralism in Theology* (1975) and *The Analogical Imagination* (1980). He contributes to several reviews and is editor of the *Journal of Religion* and of the *Religious Studies Review*.

LEONORE SIEGELE-WENSCHKEWITZ was born in 1944 in Belgard in Pomerania. From 1963 to 1972 she studied musicology, Latin and Protestant theology at Göttingen and Tübingen and gained her doctorate in theology at Tübingen in 1972. From 1972 to 1979 she was assistant at the Protestant theological seminary at Tübingen and from 1979 to 1981 *Repetentin* at the Evangelische Stift in Tübingen. Since 1983 she has been director of studies and pastor at the Evangelische Akademie at Arnoldshain. Her publications include *Nationalsozialismus und Kirchen: Religionspolitik von Partei und Staat bis 1935 (1974)* and articles on the history of the churches, of the theological faculties, of anti-Judaism and of anti-Semitism in Nazi Germany.

CONCILIUM 1983

NEW RELIGIOUS MOVEMENTS

Edited by John Coleman and Gregory Baum   161

LITURGY: A CREATIVE TRADITION

Edited by Mary Collins and David Power   162

MARTYRDOM TODAY

Edited by Johannes-Baptist Metz and
Edward Schillebeeckx   163

CHURCH AND PEACE

Edited by Virgil Elizondo and Norbert Greinacher   164

INDIFFERENCE TO RELIGION

Edited by Claude Geffré and Jean-Pierre Jossua   165

THEOLOGY AND COSMOLOGY

Edited by David Tracy and Nicholas Lash   166

THE ECUMENICAL COUNCIL AND THE CHURCH CONSTITUTION

Edited by Peter Huizing and Knut Walf   167

MARY IN THE CHURCHES

Edited by Hans Küng and Jürgen Moltmann   168

JOB AND THE SILENCE OF GOD

Edited by Christian Duquoc and Casiano Floristán   169

TWENTY YEARS OF CONCILIUM— RETROSPECT AND PROSPECT

Edited by Edward Schillebeeckx, Paul Brand and
Anton Weiler   170

All back issues are still in print: available from bookshops (price £3.50) or direct from the publisher (£3.85/US$7.45/Can$8.55 including postage and packing).

T. & T. CLARK LTD, 36 GEORGE STREET, EDINBURGH EH2 2LQ, SCOTLAND

CONCILIUM

TRACTATE ON THE JEWS
Franz Mussner

In a major scholarly work, Franz Mussner sketches a comprehensive Christian theology of Judaism and examines the Biblical and theological issues raised by the relationship between Christianity and Judaism. He argues that Judaism is a living reality which rightfully exists side by side with the Christian church.

£15

Two controversial books on a vital issue:

Feminine in the Church
edited by Monica Furlong

A selection of essays by men and women, clergy and laity, who put the case for women taking a full part in the ministry and, drawing on the experiences of the last ten years, provide a basis on which concensus may be reached.

£4.95

What will Happen to God?
William Oddie

In a trenchant statement of faith, William Oddie argues that the attempts by feminists to reform the language and liturgy of the Church are not mere surface adjustments to suit contemporary thinking, but an attack on the fundamental beliefs of the Christian faith.

£4.50

The Nature of Doctrine
Religion and Theology in a Post-Liberal Age
George A. Lindbeck

Participants in ecumenical conversations often agree about Christianity, even where their inherited confessional formulations appear to contradict one another. In a groundbreaking work, one of America's leading systematic theologians seeks to construct a new basis for Christian theology, using techniques borrowed from anthropologists to examine doctrine as the grammar of religion and drawing an analogy between being religious and learning to use a language.

£10

Jesus: The Compassion of God
Monika Hellwig   160 pp   Pbk   **£7.50**

Approaches the mystery of Christ from questions raised by the great liberation movements of our times, with chapters on: the Buddha and the Christ; Moses, Jesus and Muhammad; Jesus and Marx; Jesus and Gandhi

Infallibility: The Crossroads of Doctrine
Peter Chirico   348 pp   Pbk   **£10.50**

' ... at last ... an intelligent book on the subject ...' Bishop B. C. Butler

' ... outstanding ... depth, thoroughness and consistency ... ' Avery Dulles SJ

Sacramental Realism:
A General Theory of the Sacraments
Colman O'Neill OP   224 pp   Pbk   **£8.50**

' ... a serious offer by a studious thinker on basic theoretic issues in sacramental theology.... should have a wide reading.... many remarks in this book are intriguing; they produce a conversation with the reader.' *Worship*

A Theology for Ministry
George H. Tavard   164 pp   Pbk   **£7.50**

' ... on the practical and the theoretical levels .... carefully thought-out ... deeply in touch with the sources of Catholic doctrine and with obvious concern for the well-being of the Church ... ' *Doctrine and Life*

Luther and His Spiritual Legacy
Jared Wicks SJ   182 pp   Pbk   **£7.50**

' ... topical and helpful ... fresh approach ensures that it will be read with interest both by students of Luther and students of the theology and spirituality of conversion.' Michael Hurley SJ

Vatican II: Open Questions and New Horizons
Stephen Duffy, Avery Dulles, George Lindbeck, Gregory Baum, Francine Cardman   138 pp   Pbk   **£7.50**

Faces major topics that have developed since the Council: Catholicism's search for a new self-understanding; faith and liberation; women and laity; the American experience of Church; Vatican II and Protestant self-understanding.

The Sacrament of Penance and Reconciliation
Clement Tierney   200 pp   Pbk   **£7.50**

' ... theology is presented through five principal themes: sin, mercy, conversion, repentance and reconciliation.... provides a very helpful reflection on the meaning of the sacrament of penance.... there is a welcome stress on the biblical background of the themes treated.... contains much useful material for reflection and for preaching ... ' Bishop Donal Murray

Dominican Publications
69 UPPER O'CONNELL STREET, DUBLIN 1